THE
BEAN
BOOK

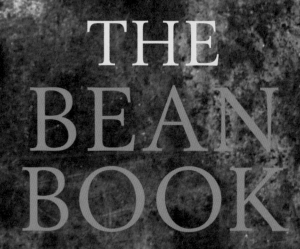

THE BEAN BOOK

100 RECIPES FOR
COOKING WITH ALL
KINDS OF BEANS,
from the
RANCHO GORDO
KITCHEN

STEVE SANDO

WITH JULIA NEWBERRY

Photography by Ed Anderson

TEN SPEED PRESS
California | New York

CONTENTS

FOREWORD

If you were a cook or chef in San Francisco in 2004, it was a special time. The legendary Rainbow Grocery Cooperative was in full swing. Tartine Bakery had recently moved to a corner location in the Mission District, up the block from the reimagined Bi-Rite Market, and was pumping out soon-to-be famous country loaves and pastries. Blue Bottle Coffee was planning to open its first café behind a roll-up door in a Hayes Valley alley. And, after years of temporary stalls in nearby parking lots, there was much fanfare surrounding the opening of the farmers' market at the historic San Francisco Ferry Building.

San Francisco mornings tend to be foggy, cold, and moody. On Saturdays, you'd find me up early, in the car not long after first light. I'd make my way past blocks of pastel-colored Victorian houses, over Pacific Heights, then banking east toward the Broadway Tunnel and on to the Ferry Building farmers' market. I was always searching for the magic, chasing the good stuff: the lettuces that glowed, the electric yellow Buddha's hand citrus, wrinkled passion fruit, ruby red alpine strawberries the size of my pinky finger. Good ingredients were king, and to have your pick of the best, you got to the market early.

This is where I first saw the beans. It's where I met Steve, and it is when I started a twenty-plus year love affair with Rancho Gordo. It was his second week there, and the tables at Steve's stall were neatly lined with brick-shaped Rancho Gordo–branded packages of beautiful heirloom beans in a kaleidoscope of hues. Their names were evocative and romantic, and each bean had a unique color or pattern and description. I immediately wanted to know all of them. At a glance, something I previously perceived as ordinary became extraordinary.

Looking back at my notebook, that day I bought: two bags of Black Calypso beans, one bag Black Valentine beans, one bag White Tepary beans, one bag Jacob's Cattle beans, and one bag White Corn Pozole.

Be prepared: heirloom beans love-bomb you at first sight. This is the first lesson learned back in my home kitchen. They come on strong with vibrant colors, quirky shapes, and bold patterns. It's how they charm their way into your kitchen. But where they *really* deliver is through flavor. It's how they win the long game, and that's what Steve has always known.

Discovering Rancho Gordo launched an adventure of discovery for me. I went home that day intent on learning the language of the bean. Wanting to understand the different types—their textures, flavors, and broths. I'd come to learn in the years since which ones were fudgy, and which ones were creamy or buttery. I'd learn which ones had whisper-thin skins and the ones that were less delicate.

Steve always says, "Cook up a pot of beans and see where it leads you." I can attest, it's typically someplace wonderful. To that I'll add another mantra I've come to believe, "Good beans will lead you to good places." Since moving from San Francisco to Los Angeles, I've had to seek out my Rancho Gordo supply from new places. You can order beans from the Rancho Gordo website, of course, but finding the small retailers stocking heirloom beans can be rewarding. Stand in front of a shelf of good beans, and you'll likely find yourself immersed in other small ingredient producers also focused on flavor first. Places like Gusto Bread in Long Beach, Alta Baja Market in Santa Ana, and Gjusta Grocer in Venice Beach all come to mind—but gold mines like these are dotted across the country.

Consider this my love letter to Steve and Rancho Gordo. He's always reminding us that cooking a simple meal for those you love is one of life's great pleasures, and cooking through a library of beans is undoubtedly a worthy adventure.

—**Heidi Swanson**

INTRODUCTION

STEVE'S STORY

If your experience with beans started with red kidney beans from a can at a lonely salad bar in a dark, old-school pizzeria, it's easy to understand your confusion about the recent popularity of beans. I remember—not so fondly—bowls of funky red kidneys, white navys, and mediocre garbanzos waiting to be paired with too-thick slices of cucumber, wilted lettuce, and over-seasoned and yet somehow bland "Italian" dressing.

Until recently, poor old beans hadn't received a lot of love in the United States. It was thought by many that they were to be reserved for hard times, were hard to digest, required hours of painstaking preparation, and were better suited to old hippies who lived on communes. They certainly weren't part of the mainstream American diet, and many of us didn't give them a second thought, except for childish chants and poems about their non-culinary powers.

Things slowly started to change.

Like heirloom tomatoes, mostly forgotten varieties of beans that had thrived under the care of experienced home gardeners started to be grown commercially and were available at a lucky few farmers' markets. Chefs embraced them and the crowds

1

went along. Home cooks who only knew beans from cans started playing with heirloom and new-crop beans—and instead of being neglected, the beans were starting to be celebrated.

It turns out that standard commodity supermarket beans are fine, but as with tomatoes, corn, or just about any vegetable, most modern varieties have been bred for yield and ease of harvesting. These are two important factors, clearly, but what about flavor and texture?

For some growers, the goal is to produce as much as possible for the lowest price. Providing a cheap plant-based protein is admirable, but life is rarely an all-or-nothing proposition. Along with the commodity beans, why not explore the history, flavor, and nuance of lesser-known varieties?

I often tell a story about visiting an agriculture exposition at a university where they were able to show off the different breeding programs they were developing. One field had all white beans, another field had perfectly round beans, and yet another had plants that were easier to harvest by machine, and so on. I asked innocently how any of these breeding programs affected the flavor of the beans, and I was met with a blank stare. In five years of field trials, they had yet to cook a single pot of beans to see if the flavor changed, for better or worse.

The contemporary thinking was that it didn't matter since you'd want to add rich chicken stock or a ham bone or another flavoring ingredient because beans on their own weren't worth much. It's similar to the comparison between acorn-fed pork from Spain (which only needs curing to be delicious) and factory-raised pork that is smothered in barbecue sauce, in part to make up for the lack of flavor in the pork. Both are acceptable, but I'm much more interested in quality ingredients and cooking them with minimal fuss to allow their natural flavor to come through.

No longer the bland, chalky kidney beans in that salad bar of long ago, the beans we have available today are gaining cultlike status, and demand for all sizes and colors and shapes continues to grow.

————————

My story with beans starts with me turning forty and almost giving up. I had been an almost-successful serial entrepreneur, and I thought I'd reached the end of the line. I was prepared to get a bad job at a big-box store and start a garden. I'd done a little gardening, and my instincts told me that if I had a garden, things would work out somehow. I was right. I started growing and taking things to the farmers' market, and I never got around to that big-box store job. The early internet was especially kind to farmers and gardeners interested in buying and trading seeds, and I'll never forget the thrill of growing beans and finally tasting a pot of Rio Zapes at the end of the season. The flavor and look was similar to the pintos I liked, but there was something extra. A hint of coffee, or was that chocolate, or both? It didn't matter. I was hooked. I quickly realized I was a better evangelist than a grower, and now my company, Rancho Gordo, works with several farms on the West Coast, in Mexico, and in Europe to bring in my favorite varieties.

One of my old entrepreneurial efforts was as a web designer, so when people really started shopping for food in earnest over the internet, I was poised and ready. I found I was most comfortable talking to other home cooks via the farmers' markets or the internet rather than dealing with distributors or big stores, so we kept the business primarily direct-to-consumer, an idea that hadn't quite taken hold when we started but now is a standard practice.

I was rather lonely when I first sold my beans at the local farmers' markets. It was the early 2000s, and in general people were kind but also felt sorry for me because I was so passionate about such a "loser" ingredient. But one by one, opinions changed. There were some hard-core bean evangelists who would tell their friends, and their friends became customers, and slowly but surely, there was an audience.

Heirloom beans are seeds that have been preserved for certain characteristics and passed down through generations; when planted, they will produce the same kind of bean every time. I surely wasn't the first person to understand their worth, but I did feel as if they were my secret and it was my job to share them with the world. There were a few attempts by other companies to commercialize them, but success was limited. And the motivation to share them wasn't focused on changing our diet. I think the talent it takes to grow beans is completely different from the talent it takes to get others excited. Farmers mostly saw them as a commodity, not the way I did. I remember being in a flowering bean field, leaves and stems waving in the gentle wind, and seeing the number of pots of beans we could provide.

Early on, good chefs were my customers at the farmers' markets. Thomas Keller of The French Laundry was an immediate fan, and others quickly followed. At the time, most people thought of beans as poor-people food or hippie food, if they thought of them at all. Keller understood that they were a perfect ingredient that had been taken for granted. They were unknown to most, but this secret was about to get out.

Soon enough we had a warehouse and small retail store in Napa. Now I look back on those early and difficult days with fondness. Wednesday was a day off, but Friday morning was the St. Helena farmers' market, and Friday night there was a great block party in Napa called Chef's Market. Saturday mornings I started in Calistoga, then made the two-hour trek south to Oakland's Grand Lake market. Sunday was the market at the Frank Lloyd Wright–designed civic center in San Rafael. Monday was off, but Tuesday was the regular Napa farmers' market and Thursday was the small Yountville farmers' market. Each week I covered more than 200 miles!

At each of these markets, I'd lay out an elaborate display of twenty different types of beans in baskets on top of colorful vintage Mexican tablecloths. At first I sold the beans in bulk, but too many people were sticking their hands in the baskets, and it was hard to ask them to stop when they were clearly having so much fun. I switched to closed bags and displayed a bowl of loose beans with a sign that read, "Touching Beans. Go ahead, you know you want to." A shot of the colorful beans and that sign (with our logo!) was very popular on the photo-sharing website called Flickr, long before Instagram was a thing.

Our sales continued to grow, and we were reaching more stores. We have never hired a publicist, but reporters still came. Writers and reporters liked discovering us on their own rather than through press releases. The *Washington Post* was the first big one. *Food & Wine* did a terrific article pairing us with San Francisco chef Laurence Jossel of Nopa. We were featured in *Gourmet* magazine, the *Los Angeles Times,* and maybe my favorite, a twelve-page article in *The New Yorker.* Each article added another level of awareness for the beans and allowed us to grow naturally.

I don't want to overstate our importance in the long history of beans, but I will say that I'm glad we found each other. It's been a great, happy relationship.

The most satisfying part of all of this is seeing a novice, with just a passing understanding of beans, buy their first bag of heirloom beans and come back and report their victory. It's the same story every time. They take these funny little stones and turn them into something exceptional to eat. It's a miracle and they can't wait to tell me about it, which is cute since this miracle happens all the time. Then the first pound purchased leads that customer to discover other varieties, and then we have a new evangelist for beans. And I still feel like doing a victory lap once a pot of beans is cooked. It's an amazing feeling, and it also means I'll eat well throughout the week.

From Napa I made it to the San Francisco Ferry Plaza farmers' market, and later we even opened a store. With such an inexpensive item and San Francisco's famous real estate prices, it was hard to make it work, but I considered it advertising. Thousands of people would walk by on their way to the famous Slanted Door restaurant, among other sites in the building, and sample and buy our beans. Our fan base grew.

You might ask, "Why bother cooking beans when canned beans are so available?" Heirloom beans can sometimes be found canned, a new and interesting twist. The reality is that canned beans, especially for some recipes, are fine, but it's recommended that you rinse them before eating because there is usually added sodium and an unappealing liquid. Once you've drained and rinsed them, you'll find wild variations in the quantity of beans. Some cans will give you a cup and a half, and others will offer much less, barely over a cup. Why pay for water that you'll have to send down the sink anyway? Besides that, the act of canning a bean changes the texture and diminishes the flavor.

A true benefit of cooking dried heirloom beans, along with the superior flavor and texture, is the bean broth. After cooking beans for a couple of hours with aromatics, you are left with essentially free soup. If you drain properly cooked and seasoned beans, the liquid you are left with is delicious. It's easy enough to make soup, using one-third bean broth, one-third chicken or vegetable stock, and one-third pureed tomatoes. Add some wilted vegetables from your refrigerator and some croutons, and you have a great soup. Another good use of bean broth is for making rice. You can replace some or all of the water for cooking rice with bean broth for an extra-rich, high-protein dish. When I have friends for dinner, I sometimes have shot glasses filled with bean broth, topped with chopped raw red onion, a pinch of oregano, and a dash of fresh lime or lemon juice. It's a hit because it's different and really delicious.

The other amazing thing about cooking beans is that when you make a pot, you aren't just following a recipe. In fact, you can gather all the tips you think you need, but you are still going to have to think on your feet, just a little. The age of your beans, the quality of your aromatics, the hardness of your water, the kind of pot you're using, and even the weather all affect the timing and flavor of your pot of beans. The very good news is that you have to work extra hard to mess up a pot of beans, and it's not difficult to make an excellent pot. The even better news is that you become a better cook with each pot you make.

Some may say this is a stretch, but I believe that when you cook beans, you're connecting with thousands of years of tradition. Your simple act links you to your ancestors and the land around you. You are safe from hunger. You are in harmony with the earth, taking care of yourself and your family and friends. You could have tapped your credit card on a card reader from a delivery service bringing you a bag or two of tepid prepared food, but you chose to do something more substantial. When you cook beans, you are almost playing with fire in the best sense. If you add a pot to your barbecue while the meat is cooking, you truly are playing with fire. It's primal and it's fun, and of course it tastes like nothing you could order for delivery from your smartphone. And *you* did it. You've done something good and substantial. Bean People everywhere, I respect and salute you.

BEANS IN THE AMERICAS

Beans have been with us for a very long time. Here in the Americas, wild *Phaseolus vulgaris*—also known as the "common bean"—have been found throughout Mexico, in the Andes, and even as far south as Argentina. *Phaseolus lunatus*, or lima beans, have their roots in Peru. Mexico and Peru seem to be the centers of domestication, and both of those countries are still major players in the production of beans. Because dried beans are seeds, and because they travel so well, they spread quickly throughout the Americas.

Without much meat available in ancient cultures, you can see how important beans must have been: Eaten with whole-grain corn to supply the right complementary amino acids, they would have created a complete protein. Had there been no beans to eat, we could speculate that the Aztec, Mayan, and Olmec cultures might not have become so advanced.

Once introduced, bean cultivation quickly traveled north where Native Americans adopted many of the same methods developed by their Mesoamerican counterparts. Along with the beans from Mexico and Central and South America, North American Natives added their own tepary bean from the Southwest to the mix. Tiny teparies thrive in arid conditions, which made them a key crop where water was scarce.

When the Europeans came and started what became known as the great Columbian Exchange, American beans were similar enough to European varieties to be assimilated into their diets easily. Lentils, favas, and chickpeas were common in Europe, and the new beans from the Americas were welcomed.

Chickpeas, also known as garbanzos, have been domesticated for at least 7,000 years, making the "New World" beans juveniles in comparison. Just as common beans from the Americas quickly took hold in Europe, garbanzos (and lentils) quickly were adapted in Colonial Latin America and beyond.

Types of Beans

The *Fabaceae* family, also called Leguminosae, is a large one, comprising several plants whose large seeds we call beans. The genus *Vigna* includes mung and adzuki beans, as well as black-eyed peas; genus *Vicia* gives us favas and the weedy vetches; *Glycene* is the soybean genus, and there are many more. Most of the heirlooms I love best—like the ones in this book—are in the *Phaseolus* family of beans and fall into four main types: *Phaseolus vulgaris*, the so-called "common" bean; *Phaseolus acutifolius*, the tiny tepary; *Phaseolus lunatus*, the lima, which takes its Latin name from its half-moon shape; and *Phaseolus coccineus*, also known as multiflora or runner beans. We've also added garbanzos or chickpeas (*Cicer arietinum*) to our list of favorite heirlooms; they are one of the most popular and versatile legumes in the world.

Easy to grow with a seemingly endless array of colors and textures, *Phaseolus vulgaris* accounts for the lion's share of my favorite pole and bush beans. Black, brown, yellow, or white; spotted, dappled, or marked with eyes—these reliable heirlooms are a pleasure in the garden and a delight to prepare and eat.

The tepary bean, *Phaseolus acutifolius*, is the Americas' smallest bean, originating thousands of years ago in what are now the Southwestern United States and Mexico. Bean historian Ken Albala writes that teparies' small size is a direct consequence of their ability to grow in the desert: their ancient cultivators, the native Tohono O'odham people, bred them for productivity in a climate that would shrivel larger beans into indigestibility before they had the chance to mature.

The original lima bean, *Phaseolus lunatus*, originated in the Andes region of South America and got their common name from the Peruvian port whence they were shipped to Spain beginning in the sixteenth century. These were large-seeded limas; the smaller version is sometimes known as butter bean or baby lima. The large-seeded, chestnut-flavored Christmas lima is another variation on the *P. lunatus* theme.

Phaseolus coccineus, or runner bean, might just be my favorite. They're easy to grow, and many of them have an overly bright, "lipstick"-colored flower. You can eat the beans in most phases of growth, from flower to string bean, and perhaps best, as a mature dry bean. There are many claims that *P. coccineus* is the oldest cultivated legume in the Americas, and with their ability to grow in both cool and warm climates, it would be no surprise. The plant sends off runners, which can be trellised or allowed to run wild if you have the space.

Native to the Middle East, chickpeas or garbanzos, *Cicer arietinum*, were one of the earliest cultivated crops in the world. There are two main types of cultivated chickpea: kabuli (pale-colored) and desi (dark brown and compact). Garbanzo beans grow much like peas, but most of the pods have only one seed. In some parts of the world, chickpeas are eaten while still fresh and green, roasted in the pods, or boiled and salted.

GROWING HEIRLOOM BEANS

Bean growing habits vary widely. Some, like tepary beans, are tolerant of dry conditions, while most others require regular watering. A long growing season with plenty of daylight hours is essential for raising beans to their full maturity, when they can be dried and saved for cooking and planting.

A warm-weather crop, beans quickly sprout from seed, unfurling broad leaves that soak up both light from the sun and nitrogen from the atmosphere. Bean plants have one of three growing habits, each straightforwardly named: pole beans are high climbers that require support; runner beans send out long tendrils, or runners; and bush beans grow more compactly, without the need for trellising. Their flowers can be white, pink, red, or blue; blossoms are followed by the development of green pods that, if left unpicked, develop beans that can be eaten fresh or dried to maturity.

Unlike so many crops that pull nutrients from the ground in which they grow, bean plants are beneficial for the soil because they transform atmospheric nitrogen into the biological form that's essential for nourishing plant life. It's not by accident that so many Napa Valley wineries plant fava beans as a cover crop while the vines are resting for the winter. When spring comes, vineyard workers till the plants into the soil as nutritious soil amendment or "green" manure.

Harvesting at Home

Harvesting and shelling beans can be a little tedious. But it's not unpleasant if you have helpers. You want to harvest the beans when the pods are dry and the beans are firm. If there's too much moisture, you can get mold on the beans; if too dry, they become brittle and the slightest touch makes the pods spring open, and then collecting the beans inside is nearly impossible.

Once you've gathered your pods, you can put them in an old pillowcase and smash it against a tree a few times or tie up the pillowcase and let your kids swat it with a baseball bat, like a piñata. The pods will split open and the beans will fall to the bottom of the sack, and then the pods can be gently removed from the top layer. Don't forget to put the pods in the compost heap or scatter them directly over your garden bed.

After you've cleaned your beans, you'll see the reality of home bean gardening. It's a lot of fun and it's rewarding, but you just aren't likely to get a huge yield unless you have a lot of acreage to dedicate to it.

Commercial Growing

The process of growing heirloom beans is somewhat cumbersome for large-scale growers, and they tend to grow only one or maybe two varieties, dedicating dozens, if not hundreds, of acres to each type. Minor variations in yield can mean the difference between profit and loss, and commercial growers can't afford to relearn how to grow each variety every season. In addition to varying climate and daylight issues, professional machinery needs to be set and calibrated differently for each variety. For all these reasons, most growers specialize in one bean, and try to make the most of it.

In the spring, beans are planted in rows, normally two to a row but sometimes three, depending on the variety. After the growing season ends and the pods have set, a tractor cuts all the plants at the base, leaving them in the fields to dry further. When the plants are at their optimal moisture level (12 percent to 15 percent), they are pushed by hand into rows. Another tractor takes this big mess and gently shoves it into a neat row. Next, a Rube Goldberg—type machine comes along and carries the row of beans and pods up a conveyor belt and through chambers that break the pods and separate the beans. The beans eventually make it over a screen that shakes wildly, removing small chaff and pebbles from the desired bean. The finished bean goes on into a holding bin while the pods pass through a blade that sends them back into the ground as chopped "green manure," improving the soil by adding natural organic matter.

The beans go through more cleaning by gravity cleaners, screens, or even sorters with an electric eye. Most of the cleaning takes place in the field, but it's that last 10 percent or so that can really make the difference. In Mexico, home cooks know to go through each and every bean and check for debris. Cooks in the States will check, but generally insist on a cleaner product to start with, even if it's a little more expensive. One thing everyone agrees on is that there's little worse than enjoying a gorgeous bowl of beans and biting into a small but nasty dirt clod or even a hard pebble.

LET'S MAKE BEANS FROM SCRATCH

We're going to make things simple: for a delicious pot of beans, simply simmer until done.

That's first and foremost the only advice you must have. Beans are funny, and bean cooks are even funnier. The act of turning beans, which resemble pebbles more than anything else and certainly nothing edible, into glorious orbs of creamy goodness is somewhat a miracle, but it's a miracle cooks have been performing daily for centuries.

When you first start studying bean magic, maybe even after a dire experience or two, you start yelling from the rooftops and maybe even try to convince everyone that your method is the best because you managed to make a good pot of beans. There's a good chance you came up with some valuable advice, but the bottom line is still the same: simmer until done.

The problem with speaking in absolutes about beans is that there are so many variables. How old are the beans? How hard is your water? How did you store the beans? What kind of pot are you cooking them in? What's the weather like?

First, I have to tell you that yes, beans can take a long time to cook. In fact, the lower the heat and the slower the cooking, the more likely you'll have a memorable bean. It can take hours, but it's not like cooking risotto, where you must tend to the dish nearly every minute by constant stirring. In fact, you can elect to cook your beans in an electric slow cooker and leave the house altogether. It's a long span of time, but it's pleasant and leisurely and, if you make beans a habit, it's something you'll be looking forward to all week.

Sourcing

The first thing you need to address is the quality of your beans. You really want to know your producer, and you really want the beans to have been harvested within two years, within one year being even better. If you live in an urban area with lots of Latinos or South Asians buying pulses, it's possible to get a good product. If you're in the Midwest and buying limas from a plastic sack at a typical grocery store, it's less likely that these beans are fewer than two years old.

The problem with old beans is that the flavor starts to deteriorate and the beans take seemingly forever to cook; or worse, they never soften. Your best-case scenario is to find a local source, which isn't always practical. There are several bean sources on the web besides ours, but Rancho Gordo's variety is the widest. Cheese and butcher shops, surprisingly enough, can be big supporters of good beans. And there's also the very good chance that your regular market understands the value of beans. Talking with the staff is one key way to let them know that you take your legumes seriously.

Prepping

Now that you have your carefully chosen beans—hopefully a new crop—you want to check them for small stones, pebbles, and organic debris. Most of the bean cleaning happens right in the field, and even with modern "triple-cleaning" technology, there's a chance there's some dirt amongst your beans. So, hunt for junk and then rinse well in several changes of water.

Soaking

At Rancho Gordo, we rarely soak our beans, unless they are the larger varieties, like Royal Corona or Scarlet Runner. We've found soaking is not really necessary when you are cooking new-crop beans. Many cooks in Mexico don't; most cooks in Europe do.

Soaking speeds up the cooking time, but of course it delays it as well, since you're not cooking, you're soaking! Soaking overnight is a common solution, but that means you're going to need to start cooking first thing in the morning. You can soak for twenty-four hours, but I've had fresh (dried beans within a year old) actually start to harden from too much soaking. My recommendation is to soak in cool water at room temperature from two to six hours if you can; and if you can't, just start cooking.

I don't change the soaking water. For every food scientist who believes changing the water will help your digestion, there's another who thinks the effect of changing the water is so minimal that it's not worth it and can potentially mean you are throwing nutrients down the drain. You will find that old-time bean cookers are rather adamant in their instructions and allow little room for discussion. If you want to soak for eight hours and then change the water, it's not the end of the world. The main thing is that you're cooking beans!

How to Cook a Perfect Pot of Beans

When it comes to cooking beans on the stovetop, it's important to choose your pot wisely. An enameled cast-iron pot, like the Le Creuset line from France, is ideal. A good stainless steel stockpot would work fine as well. You'll also want to take the size of the pot into consideration. I've noticed that beans cook better and faster if you leave a generous amount of headroom in the pot. In other words, don't cook the beans in a pot that's so small that it's full almost to the top. Give up at least half the pot to circulating, moist air.

In the pot, add about 1 tablespoon of olive oil and sauté some finely chopped onion and garlic. Aromatics like celery and carrots are welcome as well. If you're missing one of these aromatic vegetables, don't worry. Make do with what you have on hand. I've seen chefs cut vegetables into chunks, but I like mine rather fine so that they almost dissolve into the beans. Once the vegetables are soft, add the cleaned beans and enough water to cover by 2 inches, if they were soaked, and the same if they are straight from the bag. We like to pop in a bay leaf or two if we remember (and discard them before serving).

You can use the soaking water or not—whatever your instincts tell you.

Speaking of instincts, you may feel compelled to use chicken stock instead of plain water. I understand this temptation, but I suggest you resist it when you are cooking new-crop beans from a good grower. I love meat and don't see myself becoming a vegetarian any time soon (never say never!), but the fact is, you've paid a premium price for these lovely legumes, and I want you to experience them on their own as an ingredient. Beans are mild, but they are delicious, and although the aromatic vegetables we've used complement the natural flavor of beans, chicken stock might overwhelm them. The same goes for a ham hock. I love the pork-and-beans combination, and if I had a ham hock, I'd probably reach for the yellow eye beans. But the first time you cook them, I beg you to try them au natural.

Now increase the heat to medium-high and bring the liquid to a rapid boil (see page 26 for information about boiling to remove phytohaemagglutinin). Once boiling, let it continue for ten to fifteen minutes. We joke that this is the time when we are letting the beans know we love them but we are in charge and to resist is futile. Decrease the heat to low. After the rapid boiling, we want the beans at such a gentle simmer that they're barely bubbling, letting the beans cook undisturbed for hours. The lid of the pot should come off and on as needed to control the simmering. I like to do this on the weekend and putz around the house or watch a good movie while the beans gently simmer to perfection.

If you're in a hurry, make the simmer a bit more lively, but be aware that the beans might be a little uneven and you may have more bean breakdown than you want.

BASIC STEPS FOR
STOVETOP HEIRLOOM
BEANS

I've given you a lot of
little nuanced tips, but
here are the basics:

1. Check the beans for
debris, and rinse in
several changes of water.

2. Sauté aromatic
vegetables in olive oil.

3. Add the beans and
enough liquid to cover
by 2 inches.

4. Bring the pot to a
rapid boil for 10 to
15 minutes.

5. Lower the heat to a
gentle simmer and cook
until the beans are done,
between 1 hour and
3 hours.

6. Salt when the beans
are just starting to turn
soft.

Now you can pretty much leave the beans alone at this point or work on the rest of your dinner, if you're ambitious. At some point, the pot will smell less and less like the aromatic vegetables and more and more like beans. If you test one, you'll see that it's softening even if it still has a way to go. This is when I salt my beans. It's almost as if there's been a battle between the beans and me, and this is the moment of no return for the beans. I have won. I will now salt them (see below).

Keep watching the beans. You may need to add more water. Another bit of kitchen wisdom is that you need to add hot water or the beans will harden. This one is pretty much a folktale. I add room-temperature water all the time and have never noticed the beans' texture being affected. But cold water can slow things down, so your beans may take a bit longer to cook. Keep a water kettle nearby and add hot water, or use room-temperature water in a pinch.

Once the beans are finished, you should be able to blow on the surface of a bean and see the skin wrinkle. Or you could just pop one in your mouth. Beans should have some texture, but they should never be crunchy or too al dente. Test a few beans, in case there was uneven cooking or you have a mixed lot of beans.

Salting and Flavoring

You want to salt at the right moment so that there's time for the salt to penetrate the beans' interior. Otherwise, you'll just have salty water and under-seasoned beans. Traditional folklore tells us that salt toughens beans; I haven't found this to be true. I've experimented and added the salt up front and there's been no negative effect, but I still don't trust salting too early. I'm too cheap to waste a pot of beans, and after all these years of cooking beans, I just can't salt right off the bat. The other problem with salting too early is that you might oversalt, either from a heavy hand or the liquid evaporation that will happen from cooking.

If you want to add tomatoes, limes, vinegar, molasses, or some other acid, wait until the beans are thoroughly cooked. Acid toughens the skin, not to the point where the beans will never soften, but it delays the process and actually changes the texture of the beans.

MASTER RECIPE FOR POT BEANS

When you make this pot, you'll be set for the rest of the week. The night you make the beans, treat yourself to a bowlful topped with a sprinkling of chopped white onion and a dash of olive oil. I like a squeeze of lime, too. I like plenty of bean broth, but the beans should be the star and not lost in a bowl of liquid. This is good, simple cooking at its best.

At least once, make your beans this way, with no stock or pork or much of anything. I think you'll see that bones and stock are not necessary for good beans.

1 tablespoon extra-virgin olive oil or other fat

½ white onion, chopped, plus more for garnish

2 garlic cloves, smashed

1 pound uncooked heirloom beans, picked over and rinsed

1 teaspoon dried Mexican oregano, preferably Rancho Gordo Oregano Indio

Salt

4 limes, halved, for serving

Fresh cilantro, minced, for serving

Fresh serrano chile, minced, for serving

MAKES 6 TO 8 SERVINGS

In a stockpot over medium heat, warm the olive oil. Add the onion and garlic and sauté until soft and fragrant, about 5 to 7 minutes. Add the beans, oregano, and enough water to cover by 2 inches. Increase the heat to high and bring to a rapid boil; boil for 10 to 15 minutes. Decrease the heat so that the beans are barely simmering and cook, partially covered, until the beans are soft, from 1 to 3 hours. Add more water as needed to keep the beans fully covered.

Just before the beans are done, season them with salt. (For 1 pound of beans, I recommend about 1 tablespoon of salt.)

Ladle the beans and some broth into bowls. Serve with limes, chopped onion, cilantro, and minced chile.

HEIRLOOM BEANS IN THE SLOW COOKER

Every day at the Rancho Gordo store in Napa, our retail staff cooks a batch of our heirloom beans in the slow cooker for customer samples. This is the method we use, and it never fails to elicit *oohs* and *ahhs* from our customers. We love the mellow earthiness that our Oregano Indio adds, but you could substitute Mexican oregano, or leave it out. Once you get familiar with your particular slow cooker model, this is a no-fail, no-fuss way to cook beans.

1 pound uncooked heirloom beans, picked over and rinsed

2 garlic cloves, finely chopped

½ small onion, preferably white, finely chopped

1 tablespoon olive oil

1 tablespoon dried Mexican oregano, preferably Rancho Gordo Oregano Indio

1 tablespoon salt

MAKES ABOUT 6 CUPS OF COOKED BEANS

Depending on how much time you have, you can soak the beans or cook them right away. Soaking the beans will reduce the cooking time by 1 to 2 hours, depending on the bean variety. If you choose to soak, cover the beans with 2 inches of water and soak for 4 to 6 hours.

Place the beans in the slow cooker and make sure they are covered with about 3 inches of water. Add the garlic, onion, and oil. Add the oregano, crushing it with your hand first to release the flavor.

Put the lid on the slow cooker and cook the beans on high for 3 to 4 hours (for soaked beans) or 4 to 5 hours (for unsoaked beans). Check the beans occasionally for doneness to avoid overcooking. Once the beans are soft, add the salt and stir gently. Remove the lid and allow the beans and cooking liquid to breathe for 30 to 60 minutes.

A Variety of Cooking Methods

There isn't just one way to cook beans from scratch. Here are several ways to make it easy to get those beans ready for use in any recipe.

OVEN-COOKED BEANS

For a pot of simple baked beans, we recommend the Parsons Method. Russ Parsons, formerly of the *Los Angeles Times*, and author of *How to Pick a Peach* and *How to Read a French Fry*, perfected this technique: Preheat the oven to 350°F. Sort and rinse 1 pound of beans, then place them in a Dutch oven with 6 cups of water. Add aromatics if you like, such as garlic, onion, bay leaf, etc. Bring to a simmer on top of the stove, and simmer for 10 minutes. Cover the pot and transfer it to the oven to bake until the beans are done. This can take anywhere from an hour to 2 hours, depending on the type and age of the bean. Add 1 teaspoon of salt once the beans begin to soften or right at the start of the baking time, if you are brave. Check the water level often and add more hot water as needed, but try not to fuss too much. The more you leave them alone, the more successful your pot.

SLOW COOKER METHOD

Another, perhaps more practical, manner of cooking beans is using the slow cooker (see opposite page). You might want to sauté the aromatics in a pan before adding them to the cooker along with your beans and the water. I've found that slow cookers can vary in their cooking, even among the same brands. The first time you cook with yours, you'll want to be home to observe how it performs. Some run very hot and some seem a little slower.

In general, with freshly harvested heirloom beans, you can put them into the slow cooker in the morning on high and arrive home from work to a glorious pot of beans, with no soaking. Most of the newer models start at high for a certain number of hours and then switch to warm. You'll need to play with yours a bit to find the sweet spot.

The one disadvantage of the slow cooker is the lack of evaporation. They need their lids on to perform the way they were intended. So once you get home, immediately remove the lid, give the beans a stir, and allow them to breathe and reduce for another hour, if you can. This would be the time to salt as well, if you haven't.

There is an issue with phytohaemagglutinin, a natural toxin found in some beans, especially red kidney beans. You really need to bring them up to a boil for an extended period in order to release the toxins. Most modern slow cookers can accomplish this, but to be safe, a lot of experts advise bringing the beans and water to a rapid boil on the stovetop before cooking them in a slow cooker. Even with this added step, the luxury of walking away from a slow cooker filled with beans and returning to a delicious, gently cooked pot is heavenly.

PRESSURE COOKER METHOD

Perhaps the most popular technique now is cooking beans in a countertop electric pressure cooker. We don't love this method, but it's hard to argue with its popularity. The pressure cooker has really changed the way people cook and, therefore, eat. Home cooks who wouldn't dream of bothering with stovetop beans find the convenience of the pressure cooker a great solution, especially when time is an issue.

First, the good news. With either the electric countertop version or the more traditional stovetop pressure cooker that many of us grew up with, you can have cooked beans within an hour of thinking about it. That's pretty amazing.

Take your cleaned beans and add some aromatic vegetables and some oil. The oil here is for flavor, and it also prevents your safety valve from getting stopped up, which apparently can happen with some models. Add water to cover the beans by 2 to 3 inches. Cook at high pressure for 20 to 50 minutes, depending on the type of bean, slow-release the top, and then cook for another 20 minutes with the lid off, which will breathe some life back into the beans and evaporate the pot liquor, making for a better pot of beans. We'd guess that most people don't bother with the last 20-minute simmer, but we think it's what makes all the difference, with countertop or stovetop pressure cookers.

The bean texture tends to be denser than it is when they're cooked as pot beans. This isn't always a bad thing: when you're making a pureed soup or refried beans, it doesn't matter at all.

The worst part of the pressure cooker method is the bean broth. It can taste flat and lifeless, so that last 20-minute simmer is key.

When the countertop versions, such as Instant Pot, became popular, we experimented a lot. It was surprising how long it took for the pot to come to pressure, especially when compared to a more traditional stovetop cooker. It's not the end of the world, but it seemed pokey and sluggish for such a time-saving device.

Again, we know many home cooks who swear by their machines and love them.

COOKING IN CLAY

From the Middle East to Europe, and of course here in the Americas, it's amazing how many cultures and cuisines insist that the best beans are cooked in clay pots. Ask any grandmother who loves to cook and they're likely to suggest a clay pot for beans.

Low-fired clay pots can be used directly on a gas range, but high-fired pots are better for serving or using in a low-heat oven.

Of course, the lead in some glazes is concerning. Not just for you, especially with acidic foods that might cause the toxin to leach out, but for the ceramists who are working with leaded glazes. Unglazed pure earthenware pots are available and are gorgeous, perhaps working even better than their glazed counterparts.

All of the techniques mentioned earlier can be applied to clay-pot cooking, except for the high heat part of the process. Clay is a great conductor of heat, and you'll find you don't really need the extreme temperatures (unless cooking red kidney beans). The key is to make changes in the fire slowly, so that you don't shock the pot, which could crack it. When you bring water to a full boil, start on low and gradually increase the heat. (Knock on wood, I've broken only one of my clay pieces by dropping it, never from cooking.)

I even sauté the aromatics in oil right in my clay pots. Within seconds, the oil starts bubbling, cooking the vegetables as if in a frying pan.

No matter which cooking method you use, a simple pot of beans—new-crop heirloom beans—really doesn't need a lot of help. A simple, brothy pot cooked with aromatic vegetables, a little olive oil, and the slightest pinch of an herb, like Mexican oregano or thyme, is everything a bean lover could hope for.

BEAN-COOKING STRATEGIES

It may sound odd to develop a strategy for your beans, but it's not like heating up a bag of microwave popcorn. You've invested in the beans, the aromatics, the pot, and of course, your time. Instead of cooking up a pot of beans for a single recipe, let's cook up a pot of beans and see where the pot leads us. This means you'll always have beans on hand and the potential for something wonderful for you and your gang to eat.

Let's say you have a pot of white beans.

Your first meal might be a bowl of white beans with one of our topping suggestions (see page 245). The next meal, add some chicken or vegetable stock to a portion of the beans and make a soup. It can be thick and creamy or light and clear, with the beans as an ingredient instead of the base. You are in charge! Next, add some beans to a mixed green salad. Or to a salad with crunchy things like carrots, fennel, radishes, and onions. The creamy bean is an indulgent contrast to the crunchy vegetables. If there are any beans left, puree them with olive oil, a drop of fish sauce, and parsley and other fresh herbs to make a dip for crackers or crudités.

For your next pot, try darker beans and make enfrijoladas (see page 235), then make refrieds (see page 61), with the rest of the pot. Use the refried beans in a burrito or smeared on toast and topped with cheese and salsa for mollete (see page 236). It's not likely you'll have any left, but if you do, add the refried beans to stock, toss in some leftover roasted vegetables from earlier in the week, and call that "soup for dinner."

The pot after that can produce a bed of beans for roast chicken. If you're feeling especially lazy, make it a store-bought rotisserie chicken. You can get a large platter and spread the entire bottom with beans, then cut up pieces of the chicken and lay them on the beans, and then add sautéed greens, like chard or spinach, over in a corner. One platter and you've got dinner for a crowd. If you have leftover beans from this dish, add them to a mixed salad. The juices from the chicken are likely to have meandered their way into the beans, making them extra rich.

I love to cook a pot of beans on Sunday and use it as part of dinner that night. The rest goes in the refrigerator for use throughout the week.

Yields, Soaking, and Storing

You can expect 1 cup of dried beans to yield about 3 cups cooked beans. One pound of dried beans (which is about 2 cups) will yield about 6 cups cooked beans.

If a recipe calls for canned beans: one 15-ounce can of beans equals about 1½ cups cooked beans.

Rancho Gordo beans and other new-crop heirloom beans (beans sold and used within 2 years of harvest) are so fresh that soaking is not needed. It will, however, speed up the cooking time and can help the beans to cook more evenly, so if you have the time to do it, it won't hurt. We don't recommend soaking for more than 6 hours or the beans may begin to sprout.

Keep an eye on the water level during cooking to avoid scorching the beans. They should be covered by about 2 inches of water at all times. Add more hot water to the pot as needed.

Many believe that adding salt (or acids like tomatoes and vinegar) too early in the cooking process prevents the beans from getting soft. This isn't always the case, but we find it especially true with older beans.

You can store leftover cooked beans in the refrigerator for up to 5 days, and you can freeze them as well. If you are storing beans in the refrigerator, keep them in their cooking liquid so they don't dry out.

If a recipe calls for drained beans, be sure to save the extra liquid. You can use it for many things, including poaching eggs, adding moisture to dishes, and making soups.

Store dried beans in a cool, dark place. It's fine to keep them in their packaging, although some cooks prefer to transfer them to a glass jar with a lid or an airtight container. They should be good for about 2 years. After that, they are still edible but the quality will begin to decline.

Equipment

WOODEN SPOONS Obviously any spoon would work for stirring, but wood feels great and is sturdy.

TOOLS FOR MASHING AND PUREEING BEANS A metal ricer is probably the most common. It's handy and can be used for other jobs in the kitchen as well. Hard-core bean fanatics will want a wooden machacadora, which is basically a very large pestle that can mash beans and push them across a hot pan if you're making refried beans. It gives you more control and, like using a wooden spoon over a plastic one, makes the mashing a more satisfying task, but it's not mandatory by any means. As a bonus, if you make sauerkraut, the machacadora makes a great masher for cabbage.

BLENDER Sometimes you'll want to blend the beans, and a food processor or blender makes more sense. Both machines work, but we find them a little fussy to clean, and almost every time a handheld immersion blender (also known as a stick blender) is the better solution. It fits neatly in a drawer, the moving end detaches from the base for incredibly fast cleaning, and you control how much blending takes place. If you make a lot of soups, an immersion blender works well for pureeing.

THE BEAN-LOVER'S PANTRY

Dried Herbs and Spices

BAY LEAVES Adding a leaf or two of bay laurel (*Laurus nobilis*) to a pot of beans adds that certain something that makes them go from ordinary to very special. We've found that the best leaves come from Turkey. Sometimes we cook our beans with just bay leaves, a pinch of salt, and nothing else.

CANELA (MEXICAN SOFT CINNAMON) We use what is known as Ceylon cinnamon, also called "true cinnamon." It's much less harsh and has a rich, nutty flavor when toasted.

CUMIN Once we tried Burlap & Barrel's Wild Mountain Cumin from Afghanistan, we were obsessed. This varietal (*Bunium persicum*) is really different from common cumin (*Cuminum cyminum*). We use it in chili, sprinkle it over hummus, or use it in Spanish- and Moroccan-inspired dishes.

MEXICAN OREGANO There are many plants known as oregano in Mexico, but *Lippia graveolens* is the most common and is a delicious and essential part of the Mexican pantry. Mexican oregano is similar to European oregano, but less sweet and with a slight citrus twist.

MIXTECA SALT Harvested from ancient salt mines in Puebla near the Oaxacan border, this mineral is processed by letting natural spring waters evaporate. What's amazing about this salt is that it's naturally high in bicarbonates that will actually soften your beans. Add only a pinch or two at the beginning of cooking—any more and your beans could turn to mush.

OREGANO INDIO Commonly known as *oreja de ratón* or "mouse ear," this versatile type of oregano is less citrusy than the standard Mexican oregano but offers an indescribable earthiness that makes it appealing. Rancho Gordo Oregano Indio is grown by the Oregano Caxtle Cooperative in Tlahuiltepa.

SAFFRON With saffron, a little goes a long way. It adds a mellow, delicate flavor to bean soups and stews. It is the hand-harvested, dried stigma of the *Crocus sativus* flower.

SALT It's best to pick out a favorite cooking salt and stick with it. That way you know how to salt a pot of beans to your liking without having to measure it every time. We generally recommend cooking with kosher salt. It's easy to find, affordable, and consistent. If you have a salt dish filled with it on your kitchen counter, it's easy to add a pinch or two to any dish you're making. Its flakiness lets it dissolve nicely into cooked bean dishes, and its texture is great for salads as well. Flaky sea salt is the ultimate finishing salt for your beans. In the past we have imported Flor de Sal from a women's cooperative in the Yucatan that harvests these glorious "salt flowers," perfect for finishing your best dishes. If we are without Flor de Sal, we reach for Maldon Sea Salt from England or Pure Flake Sea Salt from Jacobsen Salt Co. in Oregon.

Chiles and Chile Powders

DRIED CHILES An essential part of the Mexican kitchen. It's best to purchase dried chiles from a trusted source, and the best-quality chiles generally come from Latin America or the United States.

There are many types of dried chiles to choose from, but these three are the main workhorses of the Mexican kitchen:

Anchos: The foundation. Dense, raisiny, but mild heat. Ideal for sauces.

Guajillos: Light and hot, super fruity. Nice for sauces, but not a lot of body. We like two anchos to one guajillo.

De árbol: Very hot. Mostly for salsas.

PURE CHILE POWDER We tend to prefer the bright, traditional flavor of new-crop New Mexican chiles. Rancho Gordo's chile powder is made from 100-percent ground New Mexican chiles from a small grower in New Mexico, with a medium spice, and makes all the difference when making chili.

CHILI POWDER There is a lot of confusion out there surrounding chile powder vs. chili powder. Chile powder with an *e* means pure ground chiles. Chili powder with an *i* denotes a blend of chiles, spices, and salt. It's fun and easy to make your own chili powder blend.

SPANISH PIMENTÓN Bittersweet and moderately spicy, our Castillo Spanish Pimentón is a blend of Jaranda and Bola peppers grown and smoked in Extremadura, Spain. We also love Burlap & Barrel's Smoked Pimentón Paprika, from the same region in Spain and with a similar flavor profile.

Many countries produce versions of smoked paprika, but only Extremadura has been granted the Protected Designation of Origin for the uniqueness and historical tradition of its pimentón de la vera. Students of Mexican history will recognize Extremadura as the home of the extraordinary, for better and worse, conqueror Hernán Cortés.

RED PEPPER FLAKES Favored in Italian cooking, a pinch of red pepper flakes can transform a dish. Sometimes a jar of red pepper flakes will include a mix of red pepper varieties, but the most commonly used pepper for crushed red pepper flakes is the cayenne pepper.

Vinegars and Oils

CASA STIVALET BANANA VINEGAR Fermented from ripe bananas, this lush tropical-flavored vinegar is a shock to the taste buds. We partnered with Casa Stivalet, based in Veracruz, to bring it to the United States. An excellent dressing, it can add an exotic taste to simple salads and pairs well with ceviche.

PINEAPPLE VINEGAR Essential to many Mexican stews, adobos, slow-cooked guisados, and marinades, once you start using pineapple vinegar in your kitchen, you'll wonder what life was like before it! This mild vinegar adds a traditional kick to classic Mexican food, but vinaigrette, beans, and even cocktails will benefit from this naturally fermented treat. With so many modern vinegars being nothing more than white wine or apple cider vinegar with flavorings added, it's a relief to find a vinegar fermented naturally from fruit, the old-fashioned way.

OLIVE OIL There are many olive oils (too many!) to choose from these days. You've probably heard this before, but it's best to have a bottle of basic olive oil for cooking and a bottle of extra-virgin olive oil for vinaigrettes and finishing dishes.

Other Essentials

CANNED TOMATOES Whole tomatoes, preferably San Marzano from Italy, are the best choice for slow-simmered sauces or soups. You can chop them or crush them (carefully) with your hands before adding them to your pot.

CORNMEAL, GRITS, AND POLENTA Polenta makes the perfect bed for your favorite stewy beans. What is the difference between polenta and grits? They are similar but made with a different grind and different variety of corn. In general, we use polenta for Italian-style dishes and grits for Southern cooking.

Cornmeal is also a different grind and different variety of corn, used mainly for cornbread. Yes, it's confusing!

Anson Mills grows and mills heirloom grains, and they are as obsessive about their corn as we are about our beans. They mill and ship their ground new-crop corn once a week.

PASTA If you have good-quality pasta and cooked beans on hand, you can make pasta e fagioli (pasta and beans) at a moment's notice. We've gotten the best results with shells or tubular shapes, but it's fun to experiment; try any rustic pasta, like campanelle, radiatore, fusilli, or orecchiette.

BROWN RICE Don't forget that rich, nutty new-crop brown rice also makes a great pal for heirloom beans. We love California-grown brown rice from Massa Organics and Chico Rice.

WHITE RICE Rice and beans are a classic pair, and any bean lover should have a bag of rice at the ready to complement a bowl of beans. If you can, source your rice from a trusted grower, preferably one that uses organic practices.

WILD RICE Wild rice is an aquatic seed. True wild rice is hand-threshed and most famously produced in Minnesota. You can also find cultivated "wild" rice produced in other parts of the United States, mainly California.

TAHINI Made from ground sesame seeds, tahini is a staple in kitchens around the world and an integral component of hummus. A jar of fresh, small-batch tahini can be a revelation.

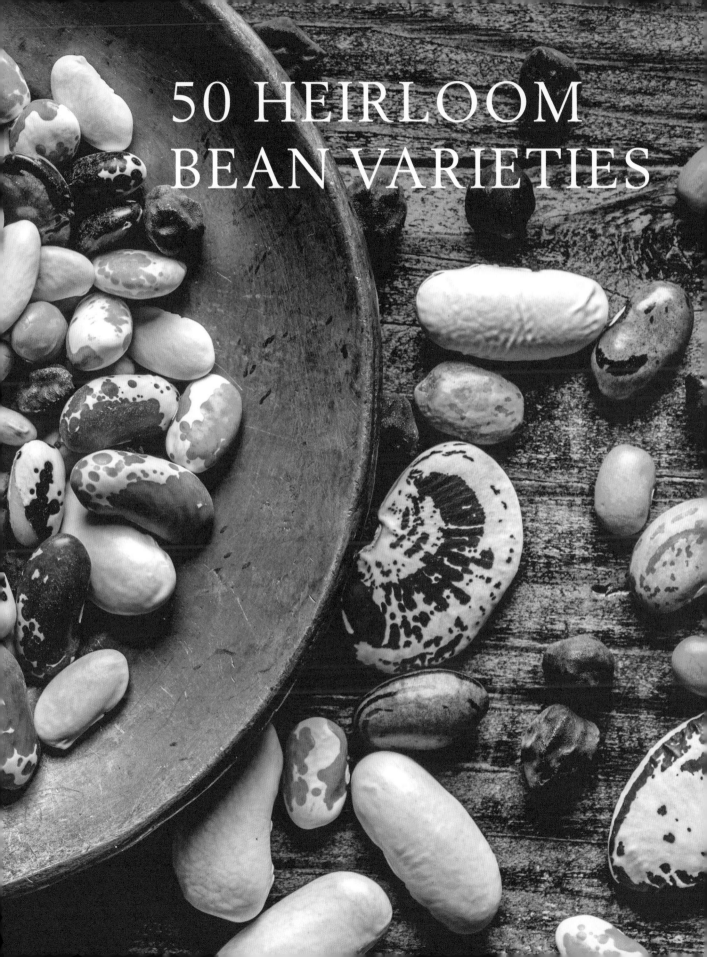

50 HEIRLOOM
BEAN VARIETIES

PHASEOLUS VULGARIS (COMMON BEAN)

1. ALUBIA BLANCA

A small, versatile white bean, classic alubia blanca beans are at home in all kinds of cooking, from Mexican to Tuscan and even classic Yankee baked beans. In Spain, *alubia* refers to beans in general. In Mexico, an alubia bean is most likely white and small.

When fully cooked, alubia blancas have a creamy, satisfying texture. The skin is thin, and the pot liquor is very good. Try starting a dinner party with a warm shot of bean broth for guests. Alubia blanca broth, with a little oregano and a squeeze of lemon juice, is just that little something you love but didn't know you needed. Use alubia blancas in recipes calling for navy, great northern, and cannellini beans. They also make a fair substitute for the rare Zolfino beans from Tuscany. They are very similar to purgatory beans, or fagiole del Purgatorio, from Lazio, Italy, as well.

RECIPE: Alubia Blancas with Clams and Spanish Chorizo, page 138

2. ANASAZI

The Anasazi were Native Americans who lived in the Four Corners area (now Colorado, Utah, Arizona, and New Mexico), dating back to 130 CE. The name is very controversial and refers to a Navajo name for *enemies*, but you'll still want these beans in your pantry.

Anasazi beans were one of the few heirloom beans available in the years before the great bean boom of the 2000s. Travelers in the Southwest often searched for the distinctive burlap sacks that held these beans. When dried, Anasazi beans have a deep reddish-brown and white speckled appearance. When cooked, the bean is pink with a mildly sweet flavor. They are similar to pinto and vaquero but lighter.

RECIPE: Roasted Cabbage Wedges with Wild Mushrooms and Heirloom Beans, page 251

3. BAYO

In Mexico, if someone mentions bayo beans, they could be referring to a general group of light-colored beans, or they could be referring to a specific bean variety, frijol bayo. Within the Bayo family are numerous variations, including bayo gordo and bayo chocolate. They are similar to pintos and Mayocobas, but slightly denser and milder.

Bayo beans are very mild, and this makes them ideal for dishes that need texture more than flavor. They tend not to fall apart, so they're good for chilis and stews.

RECIPE: Classic Charro Beans, page 148

4. BLACK TURTLE

In some regions of the world, "beans" means *black* beans. Black turtle beans have a rich, fudgy texture and inky bean broth that needs little more to make a soup. It's easy to think of them for beans and rice, Brazilian feijoada, or Oaxacan enfrijoladas, but they're also delicious in salads or chilis.

Rancho Gordo's Midnight Black bean is a classic, versatile black turtle bean that holds its shape through lots of cooking yet retains its famous creamy interior.

RECIPES: Norman Rose Tavern's Black Bean Burger, page 231, Midnight Black Bean Soup, page 122, or Moros y Cristianos, page 186

5. BUCKEYE

With their light color, people might expect the buckeye to be a little starchy and boring, so they're surprised to discover the luxurious texture this buttoned-up bean offers.

Buckeye beans, also known as Yellow Indian Woman beans, can be traced to Montana. Because of the short Montana growing season, buckeye beans have been bred to grow fast and plentifully. You can almost watch the vines grow while standing in the bean fields on a summer day.

The flavor of the buckeye is fairly mild. Their really interesting feature is their texture. You can puree them, maybe add a little anchovy or a small bit of butter, and the result is similar to eating a good triple-cream cheese without the high fat and calorie content.

Buckeyes work well in salads. They hold their shape, they're creamy, and they're a welcome contrast to the crunchier ingredients.

RECIPES: Beans Topped with Nopales, Fiery Salsa, and Onion, page 150, or Roasted Garlic, Squash, and Buckeye Bean Dip, page 69

6. CANNELLINI

Bred in Italy and incorporated into dishes in nearly every region, the cannellini bean is thin-skinned, creamy, and often delicate. Cannellini is a somewhat generic term, not unlike saying "red tomato." It can be used interchangeably with any small- to mid-size white bean, such as navy, European soldier, and white kidney, but great northern is the best substitute if you don't have cannellini on hand.

RECIPES: Italian-Style White Beans on Toast, page 71, or Tuscan-Style Baked Cannellini Beans with Tomatoes and Sage, page 213

7. COCO

A small, oval-shaped white bean that has been cultivated in France since the 1800s, the coco bean is renowned for its smooth and creamy texture and is a perfect addition to rich stews. *Larousse Gastronomique*, considered by many as the last word in French food, recommends coco for cassoulet in some of its editions. The variety known as Coco de Paimpol, grown in Brittany, has a Protected Designation of Origin.

While most beans can be used in all stages as a green bean, a shelling bean, and later, a dried bean, a lot of cooks love freshly shelled coco beans. They cook in about 40 minutes, depending on how fresh they are.

RECIPE: Classic French Cassoulet, page 206

8. CRANBERRY

The term *cranberry bean* covers a big family of beans that all display similar markings but lots of different colorations. Thought to be originally from Colombia, the bean has been bred around the world to become Cargamanto, Madeira, Borlotti, Tongues of Fire, Wren's Egg, and many more. In Mexico, you'll find them known as Cacahuate ("peanut") beans.

In Italy, there are many variations of Borlotti, but one of the most treasured is the variety from Lamon in the Veneto, about an hour north of Venice. Production of the beans in Lamon started in the 1500s. It's hard to believe that this one variation would be that much better, but it is.

Cranberry beans have a nice, almost nutty flavor and a smooth, velvety texture. The thin skins allow for a good release of pot liquor, which has contributed to their popularity in dishes like pasta e fagioli, where the liquid coats each noodle. Also consider pairing them with grains that would taste delicious coated in the luxurious broth.

RECIPES: Italian Pasta e Fagioli, page 192, or Polenta with Borlotti Beans and Tomato Sauce, page 195

9. DOMINGO ROJO

Many cuisines embrace red beans, especially when served with rice. In the Caribbean, parts of Africa, and of course in New Orleans, they're a delicious, economical way to feed a crowd. Some varieties can be waxy, and others, like kidney beans, have extremely thick skins and an interior texture that's almost like a smooth puree. Domingo Rojo beans are small, with a thick skin, creamy interior, and rich broth.

Cook them with onion and a bay leaf, then let them work their magic in your kitchen. And, of course, a rich chili with a few of these beans could change the mind of the most ardent "no beans in my chili!" chili snob.

RECIPES: New Orleans Red Beans and Rice, page 183, or Southwestern Chili con Carne, page 149

10. EUROPEAN SOLDIER

European soldier beans are one of the more traditional American heirloom beans, often used in baked beans. They have the slightest gummy texture, similar to a navy bean. Their markings might have reminded early Yankees of a soldier's epaulets, but some sources claim they look like toy soldiers. Both stories are a bit of a stretch.

European soldier is another one of the mild beans that like to soak up flavors. On their own, they aren't superstars, but in a supporting role in a dish like baked beans, they provide an old-fashioned kind of comfort.

RECIPE: New England Baked Beans, page 216

11. EYE OF THE GOAT

Known in Mexico as Ojo de Cabra, these beans are somewhat elusive; we've had a hard time growing enough every year to satisfy the demand.

These beans look interesting enough, like actual goat's eyes, but when you cook them—preferably with just onion, garlic, olive oil, water, and salt—the heavens open up, the angels sing, and you float among the clouds, filled with hope (and delicious beans).

The liquid that surrounds each bean is thick and rich without being overpowering. This is the ideal pot bean.

RECIPES: Master Recipe for Pot Beans, page 23, or Heirloom Bean and Cheese Casserole with Mushroom Carnitas, page 220

12. FLAGEOLET

Bred in France, flageolet are mostly mint green in color, with some of the beans almost white. They would be all green if growers could manage to get the entire field to ripen at the same time, which is next to impossible. A greater or lesser amount of white in the mix isn't an indication of quality. They all cook up to a light tan.

Flageolet are "the perfect companion bean." These beans have a natural affinity for lamb and fish, but their creaminess when mixed with roasted tomatoes and garlic makes for a perfect side dish.

RECIPE: Flageolet Spring Salad with Roasted and Raw Vegetables, page 86

13. FLOR DE MAYO/FLOR DE JUNIO

The bean of choice in Michoacán, Mexico, is Flor de Mayo or Flor de Junio.

Flor de Mayo beans have beautiful lilac and yellow cream colors with swirls. Flor de Junio beans have the same colorations but their markings are exotic swirls, like a 1960s silk scarf. Neither variety ages well (nor does Rosa de Castilla), and the subtle colors turn to browns and tans.

There's little textural difference between the various Flor beans—they all share a delicate, light body that welcomes pork, mirepoix, or other flavorings. They tend to be neutral and light, yet they keep their shape while cooking and almost melt in your mouth once you start eating.

RECIPE: Sopa Tarasca, page 117

14. FOUR CORNERS (ZUNI GOLD)

Gold colored with white mottled markings, this Southwestern heirloom is similar to the Anasazi, but many think it has a better bean broth and thinner skin.

There's also a variation called Raquel that is much sought-after. There's a slight chalkiness to all of them, but it's appealing. All the variations produce a very tasty broth.

RECIPE: Beans Topped with Nopales, Fiery Salsa, and Onion, page 150

15. GOOD MOTHER STALLARD

This is an all-around great heirloom bean that showcases why we bother with heirloom varieties and seed saving. This bean—prepared with just a little olive oil, onion, garlic, salt, and water—almost always knocks the socks off the lucky eater.

Good Mother Stallards are purple with really odd and wonderful cream markings of spots, lines, and flecks. Some of the beans have more cream than others, and they look like some kind of mishmash of pintos, cranberry beans, and the Milky Way at dusk. There's really no other bean quite like them.

RECIPE: Beans Topped with Nopales, Fiery Salsa, and Onion, page 150

16. GREAT NORTHERN

Nothing about this small white bean is particularly exciting, but it's a great everyday bean and can be found both dried and canned in most grocery stores in the United States. Mild and somewhat delicate, it will suck up all the flavors you throw its way.

The beans are easy to grow and often reasonably priced, so great northerns are a natural for the budget conscious. If you can find them in a store that turns over a lot of beans, they're a good choice.

RECIPE: New England Baked Beans, page 216

17. HIDATSA RED

Thin-skinned and dense, Hidatsa Red is an unusual red bean with a soft, creamy interior.

Bred by the Hidatsa tribe of the Dakotas, Hidatsa Red may look similar to other red beans, but the similarity stops there. It has a unique, melt-in-your-mouth texture and rich, beany taste. A thin skin helps make a delicious bean broth that can be used for making rice or soup, but it's not likely you'll have much left over.

RECIPE: Red Beans Tossed with Wilted Arugula and Pumpkin Seeds, page 95

18. JACOB'S CATTLE

A popular New England bean that's good for baked beans and slow-braised beans, and pairs naturally with pork. If you want an alternative to navy beans for a recipe and don't mind a tan color when the beans are cooked, Jacob's Cattle would be a smart choice. Also known as Trout beans.

Because of their very mild flavor, you'll want to pair them with stronger flavors, like a rich tomato sauce or even pesto.

RECIPE: New England Baked Beans, page 216

19. KIDNEY

Canned kidney beans can be slightly unappealing, and the fact that they are named after an internal organ doesn't help. There are many different types of kidney beans, from the common red kidney bean, ubiquitous in salad bars and chilis in the United States, to speckled kidney beans to white kidney beans (similar to Italy's cannellini bean).

As with all beans, finding a good source that turns over its stock regularly makes all the difference.

RECIPE: New Orleans Red Beans and Rice, page 183

20. KING CITY PINK

An heirloom bean from King City, California, with a rich history and a dreamy bean broth. It has a thin skin and a dense-yet-creamy interior.

King City Pinks were mentioned by John Steinbeck in his seminal novel, *Tortilla Flat*. They helped put King City, California, on the map in the 1930s, and the bean's popularity peaked just after World War II. They remained popular locally but have taken a back seat to the more glamorous Santa Maria pinquito from farther south. (Yes, we said glamorous.)

RECIPE: Sautéed Italian Chard with Beans, Corn Stock, and Crushed Nuts, page 142

21. LILA

Lila beans are a great pot bean. In the Mexican state of Morelos, they are called frijol apetito. The beans are from the south side of the quite active Popocatépetl volcano, grown mostly in arid semidesert terrain at a high altitude. They are juicy and velvety and everything you want in a bean. The raw lilac color is striking and unusual, but as with most beans, its flavor when cooked makes you appreciate what a great bean Lila is.

RECIPE: Sopa Campesina, page 120

22. MAYOCOBA

A classic bean originally from Peru, now quite at home in bean fields all over the western United States, the Mayocoba is also known as Canario or Peruano. It's a thin-skinned but meaty bean that bravely takes all the flavors you throw at it but still holds its shape.

It's popular all over Mexico, but especially in the state of Jalisco, where you often see it used for super-creamy refried beans. Use also in soups, stews, and salads.

RECIPE: Carne en su Jugo, page 145

23. MORO

A rare, regional bean in Mexico, the Moro has been seen growing near the town of Puebla (as Paraleño), but it's more commonly grown in the state of Hidalgo. It has beautiful markings and a dense, rich flavor, almost like a marriage between a black bean and a pinto but unique in its own right.

At first glance, Moro are pretty, but when you look at them up close, you really appreciate their beauty. Many beans rarely keep their colors or markings once cooked, and Moro is a perfect example of this.

RECIPE: Sopa Campesina, page 120

24. NAVY

The small, white, oval-shaped bean that's used in classic American dishes like baked beans and soups. It's said to have gotten its name because it's been a staple of the US Navy since the mid-1800s. Also known as the Yankee bean or Boston bean. They often can be quite gummy and not to everyone's liking, but they're historically important.

You can easily substitute any small white bean like a cannellini or alubia for navy beans.

RECIPES: Senate Bean Soup, page 112, or Your Black Muslim Bakery Navy Bean Pie, page 257

25. CHIAPAS BLACK (NEGRO DE VARA)

In parts of Mexico, black beans dominate. These rare black beans from the state of Chiapas are rich and dense with a thick enough skin that the beans will hold their shape when fully cooked. They are beautiful and shiny when raw, and when cooked, they are velvety and rich.

It's hard to imagine needing yet another black bean, but each variety adds a little something different. One common trait is their rich, thick bean broth.

RECIPE: Black Bean Salad with Shaved Vegetables, page 92

26. PINTO

Pintos are the classic bean: soft, creamy, and versatile. You can use them in all kinds of Latino cooking, from pot beans to refried beans. They're essential to Norteño and Southern cooking. They're the best friend a plate of carne asada has ever had.

Pinto means painted, and it refers to the appearance of the bean, which looks as if someone has decorated a plain pinkish bean with dots and swirls, not unlike the patches of white on its namesake pony. Pintos age quickly, so look for more pink and tan beans as opposed to brown.

RECIPES: Glorious Refried Beans, page 61, or Classic Charro Beans, page 148

27. PURGATORIO

Originally grown in the Lazio region of Italy, these small, round white beans are known as fagiole del Purgatorio (purgatory beans). They are delicate and mild, and best enjoyed in a simple preparation. It's customary to eat purgatory beans plain, with a sprinkle of salt and a hefty pour of olive oil, or in a simple brothy tomato sauce.

RECIPE: Eggs and Beans in Purgatory, page 135

28. REBOSERO

An heirloom passed down for generations in rural Hidalgo, Mexico, this small, compact bean is light purple, almost gray, with white or gray mottling. When cooked, it is soft and almost buttery, with a rich, soupy pot liquor that goes well with tortillas and some salsa. In their native Hidalgo, they are refried and stuffed into a masa treat called tlacoyo. Rebosero beans can be used in place of any traditional Mexican bean in recipes, especially refried beans, but they're also cuisine-neutral, so you could experiment and incorporate them into any dish that needs a mild, firm bean.

RECIPE: Sopa Campesina, page 120

29. RIO ZAPE

Rio Zape is also known as the Hopi string bean. Among the Hopi, it has been used as a fresh green bean as well as a dried one.

This is a classic heirloom bean that inspired the birth of Rancho Gordo. Suggestions of chocolate and coffee make this rarity from the pinto family one of the most popular heirloom beans.

A bean in Mexico called San Franciscano has identical markings. The size is slightly smaller and the flavor a little more subtle, but it's nearly the same bean and another example of how far bean migration can spread.

The first thing you notice is the lovely, dark purple color of the beans. When cooked, the color gets darker, almost like a chocolate-purple, taking over the black zebra-stripe markings.

RECIPE: Creamy Rio Zape Dip with Fresh Herbs, page 68

30. SANGRE DE TORO

Here is a classic red bean from the heart of Mexico. Its famous bean broth makes it a natural for all kinds of rice-and-bean dishes. A versatile red bean, Sangre de Toro (or "Bull's Blood") is also at home in New Orleans red beans and rice, chili, or just a simple bowl of beans.

Most red beans are small and dense with thin skins that exude luxurious broth. This bean is no exception.

RECIPE: New Orleans Red Beans and Rice, page 183

31. SANTA MARIA PINQUITO

There are a lot of theories about how Santa Maria pinquito beans came to California. One idea is that they were grown during the days of Father Junípero Serra, who founded—with great controversy—a series of missions up and down California. More realistically, they might have been brought to California's Central Coast by migrant citrus workers. However they arrived, it seems they're here to stay, especially in Santa Maria, a Santa Barbara County town where barbecues are elaborate affairs and pinquitos are always served.

Santa Maria pinquito beans are dense and meaty but not starchy. They don't really get to a creamy state—even with long, slow cooking—but they're a great, simple pot bean that can also tolerate a good deal of fussing, as is done at a traditional Santa Maria barbecue.

RECIPES: Rancho Meladuco's Pinquito Beans with Medjool Dates, page 162, or Santa Maria Barbecue-Style Pinquito Beans, page 164

32. SANTANERO NEGRO DELGADO

Prized black beans from Oaxaca with rich flavor and a renowned bean broth. Smaller than your average black turtle beans, these tiny heirlooms are creamy and rich. The bean broth is so distinct that the beans are also known as Siete Caldos, or "Seven Broths."

Traditional uses for Santanero beans would be enfrijoladas and lard-rich pureed beans for dipping tortillas. Because they hold their shape, they'd be a welcome addition to a mixed salad.

RECIPES: Midnight Black Bean Soup, page 122, or Enfrijoladas, page 235

33. SNOWCAP

Snowcaps are very large beans with a texture that's similar to everybody's favorite tuber, the potato. They have an old-fashioned, Yankee-style goodness that pairs well with bacon or ham, but a good vegetable base and lots of cracked pepper make them great for vegetarians as well. They have beautiful, almost surreal markings and almost look like someone dipped a cranberry bean into white chocolate.

RECIPE: Sauteed Italian Chard with Beans, Corn Stock, and Crushed Nuts, page 142

34. TARBAIS

Elusive and almost humorously expensive, even in their native France, Tarbais is a medium-size white bean. In Tarbes and nearby Camont—locales that claim the dish cassoulet as their own—they are often the preferred bean. Tarbais can stand the hours of cooking required for a cassoulet and still hold their shape.

French appellation laws make it illegal to call beans Tarbais if they're grown anywhere but Tarbes. (This is the same type of law that makes California Champagne or Oregon Burgundy a no-go.) Out of respect for the farmers of Tarbes, Rancho Gordo has been growing Tarbais seed and selling our crops as Cassoulet beans.

RECIPES: Classic French Cassoulet, page 206, or Sarah Scott's Napa Valley Cassoulet, page 208

35. TOLOSA

Alubias Negras de Tolosa are sold all over markets in Tolosa, an ancient town in the Basque region of Spain. They are prized as a regional specialty and play an integral role in Basque culture. Outside of Tolosa, they are hard to find. Dark purple to black when dried, they have a thin skin and a mild flavor when cooked. They would be at home in any Spanish-style stew.

RECIPE: Basque-Style Bean and Kale Stew, page 161

36. VAQUERO

There are dozens of "cow" beans, but we think vaquero wins for having the most realistic cow-type markings. The spots are black and white, with a slight lead going to the black ones.

Vaqueros are a classic chili bean. A good chili bean needs to be able to stand up to the fire of the chile peppers and the chewiness of the beef. Ideally, the bean would also produce a heartier pot liquor that would add to the sauce; vaqueros win on all counts.

RECIPE: Southwestern Chili con Carne, page 149

37. YELLOW EYE

Traditionally, yellow eye beans have been the variety of choice for regional baked-bean aficionados. Their russet potato texture is a perfect pairing for the other baked-bean ingredients and distinctly different from that other regional favorite, Vermont cranberry beans, which are more velvety. The yellow eye could be considered starchy, but not unpleasantly so. It's a substantial, versatile bean.

We often describe yellow eyes as a smoked ham hock's best friend. Having said that, they also shine in vegetarian dishes and simple preparations with a mirepoix and olive oil.

RECIPE: Jeremy Fox's Yellow Eye Soup, page 118

38. ZOLFINO

These small, thin-skinned beans from Tuscany have a pale yellow hue, reminiscent of the color of sulfur (*sulfur* is "zolfo" in Italian). An old Tuscan method of cooking beans is known as Fagioli al Fiasco, where delicate white beans like these were placed in an empty wine bottle with olive oil, water, and herbs and then placed in the smoldering embers of a wood fire.

Like Tarbais in France, they have their fans, but some question how much of their appeal is from good marketing. However, anytime an heirloom bean finds a fan base, we think it's a good thing.

RECIPE: Tuscan-Style Baked Cannellini Beans with Tomatoes and Sage, page 213

PHASEOLUS COCCINEUS (RUNNER BEAN)

39. AYOCOTE

Originally from Oaxaca, Mexico, the Ayocote family was one of the first cultivated crops of the Americas. They are grown all over central and northern Mexico but tend to be more popular in Indigenous communities.

Ayocote blanco is a versatile, mid-size white bean that is soft yet holds its shape through long cooking. When fully cooked, it has a creamy and starchy consistency with a mild potato-like flavor. It's a little softer and creamier than the darker ayocotes.

Ayocote morado is a large, thick-skinned runner bean with a pretty purple hue and a deep, bouillon-flavored bean broth. It's starchy but goes from dense to creamy with continued cooking.

Ayocote negro beans are very much like their purple siblings, ayocote morado. In fact, you could use them interchangeably. They tend to be a little starchier than lighter-color runner beans, but not unpleasantly so. It's not your average black bean.

RECIPES: Rancho Gordo Chili sin Carne, page 153, or Big White Beans with Roasted Peppers and Pepitas, page 88

40. CORONA

There are a lot of beans that are called corona, which means crown. They all are big, white runner beans that tend to be slightly starchy and creamy. Often, they have a thick skin but not unpleasantly so. In recipes, you can interchange coronas, Royal Coronas, and gigantes.

Corona beans can be enjoyed in salads, tossed with wild mushrooms, or eaten with just a few shavings of Parmesan and a drizzle of your best olive oil.

RECIPES: Staffan Terje's Royal Corona, Swiss Chard, and Mushroom Stew, page 131, Smitten Kitchen's Pizza Beans, page 203, or Escarole Soup with Giant White Beans and Country Ham, page 111

41. FABES DE LA GRANJA

These fabled beans are grown in La Granja, a town in the Asturias in Spain. Large and white, they are grown mostly for use in the bean-and-pork stew called Fabada Asturiana.

RECIPE: Spanish Fabada (Pork and Bean Stew), page 172

42. GIGANDE/GIGANTE

Giant white runner bean popular in Greek and Mediterranean cooking. Firm when cooked, with a creamy texture and mild flavor, perfect for slow-baked dishes. Similar to the Italian-bred corona bean and Rancho Gordo Royal Corona bean. Like most of the runner beans, their size can put stress on their skins, so cook low and slow, but not forever, unless you want a bean pudding.

Gigandes are slightly starchier than other large white runner beans.

RECIPE: Gigandes Plaki (Greek Baked Beans), page 212

PHASEOLUS LUNATUS (LIMA BEAN)

43. SCARLET RUNNER

Scarlet runner beans, in the same family as ayocote beans, are big and beefy with gorgeous markings. They are especially popular among home gardeners, who grow them for their bright red flowers, which are edible. The hummingbirds love them too, but using them only as an attractive annual in the garden seems a shame. They are large and meaty and are a good "gateway" bean for carnivores wanting to dip their toes into meat-free dishes.

RECIPE: Raw Asparagus and Runner Bean Salad, page 99

44. CHRISTMAS LIMA

Christmas limas (sometimes called chestnut limas), like other lima beans, have a distinct chestnut texture and—according to some—chestnut flavor, but it's so subtle that it's up for debate. In Italy, they're known as Fagiolo di Papa, or the "Pope's bean." Their roots most likely go back to Peru.

Christmas limas have a brick red color and milky cream markings, both of which darken as the bean ages. They may be one of the prettiest and most unusual-looking beans out there.

Christmas limas have a slightly grainy texture, and their pot liquor is rich and deep, almost beefy.

RECIPE: Heidi Swanson's Christmas Lima Stew, page 154

45. WHITE LIMA

If your introduction to lima beans was as part of a frozen vegetable "medley" of limas, carrots, corn, peas, and green beans, you'll soon learn that new-crop dried limas are a different story.

Large white lima beans have a creamy texture and savory flavor, and they taste more like fresh vegetables than other beans. They work well in baked dishes, but don't forget to use them in soups so you can take advantage of their delicious bean broth.

Baby white limas, sometimes referred to as "butter beans," are sweet, delicate, and quick-cooking. A classic Southern lima bean dish involves sautéing cooked white lima beans in butter, spices, and ham or bacon.

We prefer dried limas to fresh ones, but if you do find them fresh (or buy the frozen ones), try simmering them in some pork fat and then adding some cooked greens. If you viewed eating lima beans as a punishment when you were a child, this dish might turn them into a reward for your adult self.

RECIPES: California-Style Lima Bean Succotash, page 84, or Escarole Soup with Giant White Beans and Country Ham, page 111

PHASEOLUS ACUTIFOLIUS (TEPARY BEAN)

CICER ARIETINUM (GARBANZO BEAN)

46. TEPARY

We can't think of a bean that better represents the need to protect our heirloom varieties than tepary beans. Native to northern Mexico and the American Southwest, this bean genus is higher in protein and fiber than other beans, which are plenty nutritious in their own right. Native Americans bred the bean to be drought tolerant, so it can grow almost anywhere there's a need for a cheap, filling, healthy protein. To top it all off, it has a great flavor.

Currently in Mexico, these beans are known as Tépari and remain popular only in the extreme north. Here in the States, the beans have experienced a revival, thanks in good part to the Native Tohono O'odham nation.

When fully cooked, they have a meatiness and denseness that's not off-putting, but they're not as rich-tasting as other beans.

RECIPE: Beans Topped with Nopales, Fiery Salsa, and Onion, page 150

47. BLACK GARBANZO

Known as ceci neri in Italy, these rare heirloom legumes have a firm texture and an irresistible earthy, nutty flavor.

Black garbanzos are much denser than classic garbanzos, making them ideal for salads, stews, or even baked dishes. The skins are thicker but aren't chewy or tough, just a little more interesting.

They are not the same as the kala/black chana chickpeas that are popular in Indian cooking, but they would still shine in a curry. We thought they might be too dense for hummus, but we were proven wrong by local Napa chef Emma Lipp, who made an unforgettable hummus with them.

RECIPE: Valley Bar and Bottle's Black Garbanzo Hummus, page 75

48. CECI PICCOLI (SMALL CHICKPEA)

Small, dense nuggets of garbanzo with hints of nuts.

Quick-cooking and versatile, these small chickpeas are a well-known secret in Italy. Because they are smaller, they have more skin, which is thin, but it pleasantly changes the texture and flavor. The skin-to-flesh ratio is different, so they wouldn't be considered interchangeable with traditional chickpeas. You'll find all sorts of uses for these—from salads to minestrone to spreads.

RECIPE: Garbanzo Salad with Spanish Chorizo and Red Peppers, page 102

49. CLASSIC GARBANZO/CHICKPEA

Nutty and dense, garbanzo beans have been cultivated in the Middle East, South Asia, Ethiopia, and the western Mediterranean for millennia. They go by many names, including chickpea, ceci, garbanzo, and chana. If you are used to canned garbanzo beans, cooking new-crop garbanzos from dried will be a revelation. The bean broth is fantastic, too.

Hummus is the obvious use for them. They stay firm when cooked, making them ideal for salads and curries.

RECIPE: A Simple Hummus, page 65

50. DESI CHANA

Desi chana, also known as kala chana and black garbanzos (though they are not the same as ceci neri), are unique thick-skinned legumes with a dense, rich interior. Although similar to classic garbanzos, they aren't interchangeable. Desi chana are intense and unique and best used in recipes that were developed for them, or used as the only legume in a mixed salad.

RECIPE: Arnab Chakladar's Chana Masala, page 189

BEAN DIPS & APPETIZERS

Beans are easy to love in any form, but there's something especially addictive about them pureed for refried beans or a dip. It's almost as if your control sensors stop working, and you just can't stop eating, especially if your bread, crackers, or tortillas are tasty too.

You can make beans for a dip, but if you start each week by making a large pot of beans, as I recommend, it's likely you'll have some left over toward the end. If you have bean broth leftover too, start out with three parts beans to one part bean broth. If you have no bean broth, you can use chicken or vegetable broth, or water. Blend and check out the texture. Add a little more liquid, if it needs it.

A handheld immersion blender is ideal, but a regular blender, food processor, or even a masher of some kind will work. The advantage of blending by hand with a bean masher or machacadora is that you can control the texture. Sometimes you want a smooth, velvety dip, but other times you may be in the mood for something more rustic. You can also hold back a spoonful of beans to add to the pureed dip. It looks nice too.

Along with the beans and some liquid, you'll want to add some other components. As with the end of the pot of beans, I see this as an opportunity to use up some leftover bits in the refrigerator. A spoonful of bacon or pancetta, spring onions that are starting to wilt, the end of a jar of olives, cheese, and more can all be incorporated. Stronger flavors work because the dish will be served cold or at room temperature.

Blended beans might not end up looking very appealing. Take a cue from hummus, which is often served with a design carved in the top and then filled with olive oil. You can try this for any dip. You can also toss in chopped parsley, cilantro, or chives for some contrasting color. Raw vegetables carefully arranged around the dip can make the platter look better as well. Beans can star in other appetizers too: You can smash white beans on olive-oil-soaked rustic bread, as they do in Italy, or pan-fry garbanzo beans for a delightful snack.

GLORIOUS REFRIED BEANS

For many of us, a can of refrieds served as our introduction to beans. Straight from the can into a pot, maybe with a little oil or water added to thin them out, and they're ready to go. Making them yourself is a huge improvement, but the canned version is tolerable in a way that a can of whole beans isn't.

Once mashed, either with a traditional wooden machacadora, a potato ricer, or a blender or food processor, a bean turns into something magical. The texture, the incorporation of the onions and fat, and the pure bean taste make for a whole greater than the parts. It's no wonder they're so popular smeared on a tostada, on bread, or as a dip for fresh, hot tortillas.

If your refried beans seem too soupy because you used too much broth, no worries. Keep cooking, and evaporation will take care of the texture. If they're dry, either from not enough broth or from sitting in the refrigerator for a few days, just add a little water until you have the perfect texture.

There are suggestions to use broth to thin out the beans, but we'd suggest saving the broth for something else. They really are perfect as they are.

2 to 3 tablespoons freshly rendered lard or bacon fat, or fat of your choice

¼ white onion, thinly sliced

Salt to taste

2 cups cooked, drained heirloom beans, such as pinto, Rio Zape, or Mayocoba, plus 1 cup or more bean broth reserved

MAKES 1½ CUPS OR 2 TO 4 SERVINGS AS A SIDE DISH

In a large skillet over medium heat, melt the lard. Add the onion and a little salt; cook, stirring, until the onion is tender and translucent, about 10 minutes. Adjust the heat as needed; don't let the onion brown.

Add the beans and 1 cup bean broth to the pan. Take a wooden bean masher or a metal potato masher and, starting at one end of the skillet, rub the beans across the bottom of the pan toward the other side. The mashed beans will meld with the broth and the onion. Take your time: keep cooking and mashing until the beans become creamy and thick, and there's a clear trail when you drag the masher across the bottom of the pan. This should take about 30 minutes. You may need to add more broth as you go. Taste and add more salt, as desired.

CONTINUED

SOME BEANS WE LOVE
FOR REFRIEDS

Bayo

Cranberry

Domingo Rojo

Eye of the Goat

Good Mother Stallard

Mayocoba

Midnight Black

Pinto

Rebosero

Rio Zape

Santanero Negro Delgado

VARIATION: REFRIED BEANS WITH OLIVE OIL

If you tell your friends that you've made refried beans with olive oil, they're likely to jump all over you and tell you that the traditional fat is lard, and not olive oil. After all, that's what friends are for. Smile, thank them, and then say, "It's not traditional, but it's quite delicious—and it's vegan and vegetarian!"

One of my favorite Mexican cooks loves olive oil and uses it in everything. It's different, it's not traditional for many Mexican cooks, and it's hard to beat. It's not quite the blasphemy you have been told.

VARIATION: PUREED BEANS

It's late, you're tired, and you're in a hurry. You have just a cup of beans and broth left, and you don't feel like making refried beans, but you sure would love a schmear on the quesadilla you're making. Never fear. Here's a quick remedy.

Use a regular blender or food processor to blend the beans. To get every last bit of that thick puree out of the blender or food processor bowl, it's good to rinse the vessel with water and pour this liquid into the blended beans, stirring to combine.

A SIMPLE HUMMUS

Hummus is the ultimate bean dip. It represents the Middle East, gracious grazing, and the power of simplicity through a small bowl or plate. There are many variations, but at its heart it's pureed garbanzo beans (chickpeas) seasoned and thickened with tahini paste. When you use the best chickpeas and tahini, you can't go wrong. You can make it even more sublime with excellent olive oil, lemons, and sometimes seasonings like pimentón or za'atar. Some like a heavy hand with the tahini, while others prefer a hint. There's a school that believes the skins need to be removed from the chickpeas, but one of the best hummus spreads can be one with texture. Once you make hummus from scratch, you'll be excited to present a beautiful plate smeared with hummus and decorated with a dusting of herbs and a shallow river of olive oil.

There was a trend a few years ago to call any pair of pants that wasn't jeans "khakis." Another dubbed any cocktail served in a V-shaped cocktail glass a "martini." *Hummus* is an actual word for an actual thing: it means "chickpeas." Calling any bean dip— white, medium, or dark—"hummus" is not appreciated by most hummus-loving cultures. And tahini is essential!

3 cups cooked, drained garbanzo beans, plus some bean broth reserved

3 tablespoons good-quality tahini, or to taste

2 tablespoons fresh lemon juice, or to taste

3 garlic cloves, minced

½ teaspoon salt, or to taste

Extra-virgin olive oil, to top

Spanish pimentón (smoked paprika) or za'atar (optional)

Sliced raw vegetables or pita for serving

MAKES ABOUT 2 CUPS

Reserve a handful of garbanzos for garnish, then add the rest to a food processor with the tahini, lemon juice, garlic, and salt. Pulse until smooth, adding a little bean broth if needed to loosen the mixture. Taste and adjust the salt, tahini, and lemon to your liking. You can also mix the hummus in a bowl using an immersion blender (my preferred method).

Pour the hummus into a shallow bowl and with your (clean!) finger draw a little pattern on top. Gently drizzle your best extra-virgin olive oil over the top, letting it flow as it may. Dust with pimentón, if desired, and dot with the reserved whole garbanzos. Serve with raw vegetables or pita.

WHITE BEAN AND ANCHOVY DIP

White beans and anchovies are a surprise hit. You can use just a touch of anchovy or go wild and use several fillets. If you have only half a cup of beans, cut back the other ingredients accordingly, or better yet, experiment. You may find you like more cheese or anchovies and fewer capers. This is a fun exercise in making a dip your own.

Keep a jar of good-quality anchovies in your refrigerator and you'll always have a secret flavor-booster for salad dressings, pasta sauces, pizza, and of course, beans. We've fallen for wild-caught European anchovies, filleted and packed by hand, from Donostia Foods in Spain.

Another delicious use for pureed beans is as a sauce for a bed of steamed or roasted vegetables. Or spread it out on a plate and add a roasted chicken breast, poached or grilled fish, charred vegetables, or whatever is on hand.

1½ cups cooked, drained white beans, such as Rancho Gordo Cassoulet or Ayocote Blanco beans (see Note)

2 anchovy fillets

1 tablespoon capers

1 tablespoon pineapple vinegar or other light vinegar

1 tablespoon olive oil, or more if needed, plus more for drizzling on top

3 tablespoons freshly grated Parmesan cheese

Salt and freshly ground pepper

2 tablespoons minced fresh thyme or parsley

Sliced bread, crackers, or veggies for serving

MAKES ABOUT 1 CUP

In a blender or food processor, puree the beans, anchovies, capers, and pineapple vinegar. Slowly add the olive oil, a bit at a time, until you reach the desired consistency. Stir in the Parmesan. Season to taste with salt and pepper (you may not need salt). Transfer to a bowl and top with the thyme and drizzle with olive oil. Serve with your favorite bread, crackers, or veggies.

Note: You can try this with any medium-bodied bean that you have available. Buckeye beans would make for an especially unusual and delicious dip.

VEGETARIAN VARIATION

Instead of anchovies, add ¼ cup pitted green or Kalamata olives and 1 small garlic clove, chopped.

CREAMY RIO ZAPE DIP
WITH FRESH HERBS

The Big Game, whatever the sport, is a chance to lay out some great grazing food. There are some traditional things, like canned pinto bean dip, that could be elevated just a bit and become something great.

Dark beans like Rio Zape are just as useful in dips as white beans, but they are a little weird-looking to serve. Make sure you have lots of parsley or chives on hand to add some color.

2 tablespoons olive oil

½ yellow onion, very thinly sliced

2 garlic cloves, minced

1 cup cooked, drained Rancho Gordo Rio Zape beans or other dark heirloom beans, plus ¼ to ½ cup bean broth reserved

1 tablespoon of your favorite hot sauce (we like Rancho Gordo Felicidad hot sauce), or to taste

2 tablespoons sour cream

½ teaspoon salt, or more to taste

¼ cup cooked ground sausage or chorizo (optional)

2 tablespoons minced fresh cilantro, parsley, or chives

Sliced raw vegetables, crackers, or chips for serving

MAKES ABOUT 2 CUPS

In a medium skillet over medium-low heat, warm the olive oil. Add the onion and garlic and sauté until translucent, 5 to 7 minutes. Add the beans and ¼ cup of broth, the hot sauce, sour cream, and salt.

Using a food processor, immersion blender, or blender, blend the mixture until smooth. Taste and adjust the seasonings, adding more broth, hot sauce, and salt, if desired. Add the sausage (if using), and stir. Chill for at least 2 hours.

When ready to serve, scoop into a serving bowl or platter and sprinkle the cilantro over the top. Serve with vegetables, crackers, or chips.

ROASTED GARLIC, SQUASH, AND BUCKEYE BEAN DIP

If you'd like to incorporate or experiment with more ingredients native to the Americas, beans, chiles, and squash are a perfect starting point. This dip, inspired by the food blog *The First Mess*, employs some of the best of the fall harvest: butternut squash, chipotle chiles, and pumpkin seeds. The finished dip would benefit from some colorful garnishes, like chopped red onion and herbs.

1 small head garlic

1 small butternut or other winter squash, halved lengthwise, seeds removed

½ cup olive oil

Salt and freshly ground pepper

1½ cups cooked, drained Rancho Gordo Buckeye beans or black beans, such as Rancho Gordo Midnight Black beans

1 or 2 chipotles in adobo, depending on taste, plus 1 tablespoon adobo sauce

2 teaspoons pineapple vinegar or red wine vinegar

Roasted pumpkin seeds for garnish

Minced red onion for garnish

Minced fresh herbs, such as cilantro, for garnish

Chips or sliced raw vegetables for serving

MAKES ABOUT 2 CUPS

Preheat the oven to 400°F.

Cut the top ¼ inch off of the head of garlic. Set the halved squash, cut sides facing up, on a baking sheet. Add the garlic head, cut side up. Drizzle the cut squash and the exposed top of the garlic head with 1 to 2 tablespoons of the olive oil. Season with salt and pepper. Wrap the garlic head in aluminum foil and flip the squash over so that the cut sides are facing down. Transfer to the oven and roast until the garlic and squash are tender, about 25 minutes for the garlic and about 40 minutes for the squash. Set the squash and garlic aside to cool.

Once the squash is cool enough to handle, scoop out the flesh and measure roughly 1 cup of the cooked squash (reserve the rest for another use). Remove the head of garlic from its foil wrapping.

In a food processor, combine the squash, beans, chipotles, adobo sauce, pineapple vinegar, and salt and pepper to taste. Squeeze the bulbs of roasted garlic into the food processor.

Pulse a few times until you have a slightly chunky paste. Scrape down the sides with a spatula to make sure the mixture is evenly pureed. With the motor running, slowly add the remaining olive oil through the feed tube. Puree until smooth.

Check the dip for seasoning and adjust as necessary. Scoop the dip into a serving bowl and garnish with pumpkin seeds, red onion, and fresh herbs. Serve with chips or vegetables for dipping.

ITALIAN-STYLE WHITE BEANS ON TOAST

Marcella Hazan and I became online buddies after I noticed, to my great surprise, that she had placed an online order from Rancho Gordo. At one point, I asked her what beans she missed most from Italy. She wrote back immediately that she missed Sorana, a cannellini bean I'd never heard of.

Then, on a trip to Sorana, Italy, just outside Lucca, I met with some bean growers and learned more about the Sorana bean. My perfect Italian lunch that day started with beans served on toast saturated with olive oil, topped with a thin slice of lardo, a preserved seasoned pork fatback.

Back in the States, we found Sorana bean seeds through some sleuthing and luck, and now we grow it on the West Coast. It's one of our most popular beans, and we named it after Marcella—a tribute to a mighty force in nature.

Lardo can be difficult to find outside of Italy, but prosciutto is a great substitute. The toasts can also be served without meat, drizzled with olive oil, and sprinkled with fresh herbs, salt, and pepper.

8 large ½-inch slices country-style bread

2 garlic cloves, peeled and halved

4 tablespoons extra-virgin olive oil, plus more for finishing

6 cups cooked, drained white beans, such as Rancho Gordo Marcella or Alubia Blanca beans

Flaky sea salt and freshly ground pepper

4 ounces lardo or prosciutto, thinly sliced (optional)

Minced fresh herbs and shaved Parmesan cheese for garnish (optional)

MAKES 8 APPETIZER SERVINGS

Toast or grill the bread. Rub one side of each slice with the cut sides of the garlic, then brush with the olive oil.

Spoon about ½ cup beans onto each toast, and coarsely crush with a fork. Divide the remaining whole beans among the toasts (about ¼ cup per toast). Season with sea salt and pepper, and drizzle with olive oil. Top with the lardo, fresh herbs, and Parmesan, if desired.

PAN-FRIED GARBANZOS WITH SPICES

Hosting a dinner party can be stressful, but if you start things out with something to drink and a little food, the crowd is much more forgiving and the chef is more relaxed.

Save these delectable garbanzos for the last minute. Pass them around and then take your time with the rest of the meal.

1 teaspoon garlic powder

1 teaspoon dried Mexican oregano, preferably Rancho Gordo Oregano Indio

1 teaspoon pure chile powder or Rancho Gordo Stardust Dipping Powder

1 teaspoon salt, or to taste, and freshly ground pepper

3 tablespoons extra-virgin olive oil

2 cups cooked, drained garbanzo beans, patted dry

MAKES 4 TO 6 APPETIZER SERVINGS

In a small bowl, combine the garlic powder, oregano, chile powder, and salt and pepper to taste. Set aside.

In a small skillet, warm the olive oil over medium-high heat. Add the beans and sprinkle the spice mixture over the top. Cook, shaking the pan occasionally, until most of the moisture is gone, about 7 minutes.

Drain the beans on a paper towel. Taste and adjust the seasonings as needed. Serve at room temperature.

VALLEY BAR AND BOTTLE'S BLACK GARBANZO HUMMUS

Black garbanzos are a little heavier and denser than their more popular counterpart. It's easy to use them in salads and soups, but they might seem to be an odd choice for hummus. Yet it turns out they are a delicious option, as shown here by Valley Bar and Bottle's chef, Emma Lipp. This is a dish she created for a celebration dinner for Rancho Gordo's twentieth anniversary in 2021, and we make it often. The key here is to really puree the dip thoroughly; rustic texture is best saved for other dishes.

4 cups cooked, drained Rancho Gordo black garbanzo beans or classic garbanzo beans, plus 1 cup bean broth reserved (see Note)

¼ cup good-quality tahini

1 tablespoon Garlic Confit, or more to taste (recipe follows)

Extra-virgin olive oil

Salt

2 tablespoons fresh lemon juice, or to taste

Ice water for thinning

Toasted black sesame seeds or nigella seeds for garnish

Sliced raw vegetables, crackers, or pita bread for serving

MAKES ABOUT 3 CUPS

In a blender or food processor, combine the garbanzos with about ½ cup of bean broth (plus more if needed), the tahini, at least 1 tablespoon of the garlic confit and its oil, a glug of olive oil, a sprinkle of salt, and the lemon juice. Blend. Add a little bit of ice water to help smooth the hummus to a creamy consistency. Taste and adjust the seasoning to your liking.

To plate, spoon the hummus into a bowl or dish, then turn the spoon up, using the backside to create a channel in the hummus. Pour olive oil into this impression, and sprinkle sesame seeds to garnish. Serve with vegetables, crackers, or pita bread.

Note from Chef Emma Lipp: This is more of a method than a recipe, and it can be batched accordingly in size and in personal variations. A strong blender, such as a Vitamix, is recommended, but a food processor can work as well. Be sure to soak the garbanzos for 6 to 8 hours or overnight. Do not skip this step.

CONTINUED

GARLIC CONFIT

1 head garlic, cloves peeled

½ cup neutral oil, such as
rice bran

MAKES ½ CUP

In a small pot, cover the garlic with the oil.

Bring to a low boil on the stove, then decrease the heat to very low
to maintain a bare simmer. Let the garlic cook low and slow until
soft, at least 1 hour. Let cool.

Transfer the garlic and cooking oil to a glass jar with a lid, making
sure the cloves are submerged in the oil, and refrigerate for up to
2 weeks.

BEAN SALADS

Serving beans as the base of a salad or as part of a mixed salad can be an especially good way to enjoy them in hot weather when you don't feel like cooking. Beans make a salad more substantial, and there's the appeal of the creamy beans contrasting with the crunch of raw vegetables. The combination feels and tastes much more indulgent than it is. You could even smother the salad in a creamy dressing, and it will still be refreshing.

As much as we love bean broth, it doesn't belong in a salad. Make sure your beans are well drained. As soon as you have the inkling, let your beans strain in some type of colander as you make the rest of the ingredients.

To take your salads to the next level, let the beans and crunchy ingredients relax in a good dressing before serving. Reserve the lettuce, which will get saturated and limp if dressed too early, and add it just before serving. The only caveat is that we recommend cooling salad beans before dressing them so they don't lose their creaminess. Cooked and cooled beans, even when resting for an hour or so in a dressing, still taste and feel like beans. There's no stodginess or heaviness. They're just about perfect.

Remember you can make the dressing in the salad bowl, add the ingredients, and then toss. For a simple dressing, start by mashing salt and garlic in the bottom of the bowl, then add vinegar and grainy mustard, and finally drizzle in olive oil, whisking until incorporated.

ITALIAN TUNA AND WHITE BEAN SALAD

Good oil-packed tuna is an indulgence worth giving in to. Because this salad has so few ingredients, be sure each component is a worthy part of this classic dish. This salad begs to be eaten al fresco with good bread and sharp white wine.

2 tablespoons fresh lemon juice or light vinegar, such as pineapple vinegar, or more to taste

1 garlic clove, minced

3 tablespoons extra-virgin olive oil, or more to taste

Salt and freshly ground pepper

4 cups cooked, drained Rancho Gordo Marcella or Royal Corona beans, or other white beans, such as corona or cannellini

One 6½-ounce can tuna packed in olive oil, drained and flaked

½ medium red onion, finely chopped

1 teaspoon grated lemon zest

¼ cup chopped fresh Italian parsley or oregano, for garnish

MAKES 4 SERVINGS

In a large bowl, whisk together the lemon juice, garlic, and olive oil until emulsified, then season with salt and pepper. Add the beans, tuna, and onion and gently toss together to coat with the dressing. Taste and adjust with more oil or lemon juice as needed.

Before serving, gently stir in the lemon zest and garnish with the parsley. Serve at room temperature or slightly chilled.

CALIFORNIA-STYLE LIMA BEAN SUCCOTASH

If you don't have the burden of Southern traditions, there's a good chance this salad will be a favorite, even for those with the idea that they don't like lima beans. But heirloom limas are different. In summer, when corn, herbs, and tomatoes are abundant and at their best, you'll crave this combination of flavors. Bacon is great, but pancetta can make this salad even better.

We prefer this salad with cherry tomatoes, but any ripe, in-season tomatoes will do.

2 tablespoons olive oil or butter

4 ounces pancetta or bacon, cubed or chopped (optional)

½ white onion, minced

1 to 2 serrano or jalapeño chiles, seeded and minced

2 cups corn kernels, from 2 to 3 ears of corn

2 cups cooked, drained Rancho Gordo Large White Lima beans or baby lima beans

1½ cups chopped tomatoes (about 1 pound)

Coarse salt and freshly ground pepper

Fresh lime juice or pineapple vinegar to taste

½ cup thinly sliced fresh cilantro, basil, or mint (or a mixture)

3 tablespoons Mexican Cotija or feta cheese (optional)

MAKES 4 SERVINGS

In a medium skillet over medium-low heat, warm the olive oil or butter. If using pancetta: Cook the pancetta until it's browned and chewy, 10 to 15 minutes. If using bacon: Omit the oil or butter and cook, stirring, over medium-low until the fat has rendered and the bacon is crisp, about 10 minutes. Using a slotted spoon, remove the pancetta or bacon and set aside. Add the onion and sauté until softened, about 5 minutes. Add the chiles and corn, cover, and cook, stirring occasionally, until the corn is tender, about 5 minutes. Gently stir in the beans, tomatoes, and pancetta (if using); cook until heated through, 3 to 5 minutes. Taste and season with salt and pepper.

While still warm, transfer the mixture to a platter. Add lime juice to taste, stirring gently to combine. Taste and adjust the seasonings. Top with the fresh herbs and cheese (if desired) and serve.

VARIATION: TRADITIONAL SOUTHERN SUCCOTASH

In the American South, succotash is commonly made with fresh baby limas, bacon, tomatoes, corn, and basil. To make a more traditional Southern version, use bacon and omit the fresh chile and Cotija cheese. Garnish with fresh basil.

FLAGEOLET SPRING SALAD WITH ROASTED AND RAW VEGETABLES

Rich, roasted cherry tomatoes, lemon-zested flageolet beans, and crisp radishes say spring like bunnies and daffodils. These beans would feel right at home at a spring lunch or brunch, but they'd also make a good light dinner, especially when the first really good cherry tomatoes show up in the markets.

12 ounces cherry tomatoes, halved

5 sprigs thyme, leaves stripped from stems, plus more for garnish

Salt

2 tablespoons extra-virgin olive oil, plus ¼ cup

4 garlic cloves, unpeeled

6 cups cooked, drained Rancho Gordo Flageolet beans or other white beans, such as alubia blanca, cannellini, or navy

1 small red onion, finely chopped

1 bunch fresh Italian parsley, finely chopped

1 teaspoon grated lemon zest

1 to 2 lemons for juicing

Freshly ground pepper

1 bunch fresh radishes, cleaned and thinly sliced with a mandoline or vegetable peeler

MAKES 6 TO 8 SERVINGS

Preheat the oven to 250°F.

Arrange the tomatoes, cut side up, on an ungreased rimmed baking sheet. Sprinkle with the thyme leaves and a pinch of salt, and drizzle with the 2 tablespoons olive oil. Add the garlic cloves to the baking sheet. Bake for 1 to 1½ hours, until the tomatoes are slightly shriveled but not dry. Allow to cool. Roughly chop the tomatoes. Squeeze the garlic cloves out of their peels and chop.

In a serving bowl, toss the beans with the tomatoes, garlic, onion, parsley (reserve a bit for garnish, if desired), and the remaining ¼ cup olive oil (or just enough oil to coat everything). Add the lemon zest and the juice of 1 lemon and check for tartness. It should be very lemony. Add more lemon juice as desired.

Add salt and pepper to taste. Just before serving, add the radish slices, thyme, and reserved parsley, if desired. Toss again and serve.

BIG WHITE BEANS WITH ROASTED PEPPERS AND PEPITAS

This is a mixed pepper salad with goat cheese and beans for a little creaminess and roasted pepitas (pumpkin seeds) for a meaty texture and nutty flavor.

Roasted peppers aren't hard to make, but there's no crime in having a jar of prepared red peppers in your pantry. Jarred poblano peppers don't seem to be a thing, but once you get the hang of roasting peppers, it's no bother.

2 cups roasted poblano chile strips (from 1 large or 2 medium poblanos; see page 270 for roasting instructions)

2 cups roasted red bell peppers (store-bought or roasted, see page 270), cut into squares

½ white onion, finely chopped

3 to 4 cups cooked, drained big white beans, such as Rancho Gordo Royal Corona or Ayocote Blanco

1 teaspoon dried Mexican oregano, preferably Rancho Gordo Oregano Indio

Extra-virgin olive oil to taste

Pineapple vinegar or other mild vinegar, or fresh lime juice to taste

Salt and pepper to taste

1 cup roasted pepitas

¼ cup crumbled fresh goat cheese (optional)

MAKES 4 SERVINGS

In a large serving bowl, combine the poblano peppers, roasted red bell peppers, onion, and beans. Add the oregano, crushing it between your fingers. Stir well. Season to taste with olive oil, pineapple vinegar, and salt and pepper.

Just before serving, sprinkle the dish with roasted pepitas and goat cheese, if desired.

SUMMERTIME WHITE BEAN
AND TOMATO PANZANELLA

Any white bean would work with this delicious salad, and really, the point is to create something wonderful out of leftover bread. If you have only smaller beans, like cannellini or alubia blancas, by all means use those.

1½ pounds ripe heirloom tomatoes, cut into bite-size chunks

2 cups cooked, drained white beans, such as Rancho Gordo Royal Corona, Large White Lima, or Cassoulet beans, or any large white bean

¼ small red onion, minced (about 2 tablespoons)

1 garlic clove, minced

1 to 2 tablespoons red wine vinegar or pineapple vinegar

5 tablespoons extra-virgin olive oil

1 teaspoon salt, plus more to taste

Freshly ground pepper

About 4 cups Homemade Croutons (page 267)

2 tablespoons finely chopped fresh basil or parsley

MAKES 4 SERVINGS

In a serving bowl, combine the tomatoes, beans, onion, garlic, red wine vinegar, 3 tablespoons of the olive oil, the salt, and a few grinds of pepper. Allow to sit for at least 30 minutes or up to 2 hours.

Fold the croutons and basil into the salad, then taste and adjust the seasonings and drizzle in the remaining olive oil. Serve immediately.

BLACK BEAN SALAD WITH SHAVED VEGETABLES

You'll notice that except for the beans, this salad is all crunch. The biggest advantage is that you can make and even dress this salad ahead. Most of these vegetables can hang out in your refrigerator much longer than lettuce.

Mandolines should be used with caution and respect. You can also try shaving vegetables with a vegetable peeler, and of course, good knife skills are always handy. You will want to avoid large chunks of raw fennel for most people. The anise flavor can be overwhelming, even when dressed.

FOR THE VINAIGRETTE

1 garlic clove, minced

½ teaspoon salt

1 teaspoon Dijon mustard

1 teaspoon dried Mexican oregano, preferably Rancho Gordo Oregano Indio

2 tablespoons fresh lemon juice or your favorite vinegar

½ cup extra-virgin olive oil

2 cups cooked, well drained Rancho Gordo Ayocote Negro or Negro de Vara beans, or other black beans

4 radishes, thinly sliced

2 celery stalks, thinly sliced

1 large carrot, thinly sliced

1 medium fennel bulb, trimmed and thinly sliced with a mandoline

¼ white onion, minced

Salt and freshly ground pepper

MAKES 4 SERVINGS

To make the vinaigrette: In a large salad bowl, make a paste with the garlic and salt. Add the mustard, oregano, and lemon juice. Mix well. Whisk in the olive oil slowly.

Add the beans, radishes, celery, carrot, fennel, and onion to the salad bowl. Gently toss to combine. Season to taste with salt and pepper.

TINNED SEAFOOD TOSSED WITH WARM BEANS AND HERBS

With good reason, tinned seafood is more popular than ever. What could be easier than gently warming up a pan with a little olive oil and seafood and then tossing in some previously cooked beans? There are more brands and varieties available than ever, so this will be a fun dish to explore. We suggest trying squid or octopus for this recipe. The seafood will be cooked perfectly, often in its own ink. Essentially, you're getting a protein and a sauce from one small tin. Like most canned sauces, a gentle reheating, a splash of olive oil, and a squeeze of fresh lemon can do wonders here.

2 tablespoons olive oil

¼ white onion, minced

2 garlic cloves, minced

One 4-ounce tin squid or octopus in ink, or other favorite tinned seafood, such as sardines, tuna in olive oil, or mussels

2 cups cooked, drained white beans, such as Rancho Gordo Cassoulet or Caballero beans, plus some bean broth reserved

Salt and pepper to taste

Handful of minced fresh herbs, such as parsley or oregano

Fresh lemon juice to taste

Crusty bread or tostadas for serving

MAKES 2 SERVINGS

In a medium pan, heat the olive oil over medium heat. Add the onion and cook until translucent, about 5 minutes. Add the garlic and cook for another minute or so. Add the squid and ink and cook to warm through, 2 to 4 minutes. Gently stir in the beans and some broth. Decrease the heat to low and simmer until the liquid has reduced, about 10 minutes.

Sprinkle with salt and pepper, fresh herbs, and lemon juice to taste. Serve with crusty bread or on tostadas.

RED BEANS TOSSED WITH WILTED ARUGULA AND PUMPKIN SEEDS

Arugula, sun-dried tomatoes, and chicken Marbella all seem like things stuck in the 1980s when some of us were just discovering the power of being a home cook. Too often now we laugh at or neglect these foods, and it's a shame. They can be delicious!

Arugula (also known as rocket) is a flavor-packed green that doesn't need to be cooked, but its nuttiness comes out when tossed with hot beans. This easy side dish can be made with whatever beans you have on hand.

2 tablespoons extra-virgin olive oil

3 garlic cloves, thinly sliced

2 cups cooked, drained red beans, such as Rancho Gordo Hidatsa Red or Domingo Rojo, plus about ¼ cup bean broth reserved

4 cups firmly packed baby arugula, rinsed and drained well

½ red onion, minced

1 tablespoon fresh lemon juice

Coarse salt and freshly ground pepper

¼ cup pumpkin seeds, toasted

2 to 4 Poached Eggs (optional; page 267)

MAKES 2 SERVINGS

Heat the olive oil in a large skillet over medium heat. Add the garlic and cook, stirring constantly, until it's fragrant but not browned, 2 to 3 minutes. Add the beans and broth and stir to combine. Add the arugula and onion and cook, stirring constantly, until the arugula is slightly wilted, 1 to 2 minutes. Add the lemon juice and cook, stirring constantly, for about 1 minute. Season to taste with salt and pepper.

Divide among 2 bowls and serve immediately, topped with the pumpkin seeds and poached eggs (if using).

PINQUITO BEAN SALAD WITH ANCHOVIES, CELERY, AND LEMON

Celery is essential as an aromatic when starting broths, beans, and soups, and it's popular over the holidays for stuffings and turkey. But this fibrous vegetable can be otherwise neglected. It has a very particular taste and may not seem so versatile, but it is. Celery is one of those vegetables that really shines when purchased at a farmers' market or specialty food store. In a salad, for instance, it can be the star. Don't forget to use the leaves as well. Here, celery stands in for lettuce and adds crunch and texture.

2 cups cooked, well drained firm, medium-bodied beans, such as Rancho Gordo Santa Maria Pinquito, King City Pink, or Buckeye

3 celery stalks, chopped into bite-size pieces, plus leaves for garnish

¼ cup extra-virgin olive oil

Juice of 1 lemon (2 to 3 tablespoons)

1 anchovy

1 teaspoon fresh or dried thyme, or to taste

1 garlic clove

Salt and pepper to taste

MAKES 2 MAIN DISH SERVINGS, OR 4 SIDE DISH SERVINGS

In a serving bowl, toss the beans with the celery.

In a food processor or blender, add the olive oil, lemon juice, anchovy, thyme, garlic, and salt and pepper and blend well. If using a mortar and pestle, start with the salt and garlic and make a paste. Add the anchovy and continue pounding until the anchovy is incorporated into the paste. Add the lemon juice, thyme, and pepper and continue pounding gently until incorporated. Slowly whisk in the olive oil until emulsified.

Pour the dressing over the bean mixture and toss gently. Garnish with celery leaves and serve.

RAW ASPARAGUS AND RUNNER BEAN SALAD

This substantial salad, inspired by one in Joshua McFadden's *Six Seasons*, is a springtime favorite. The fresh mint and bread crumbs are essential, along with slicing the raw asparagus very thin. This salad is best when the first local asparagus arrive. Later in the season, no matter how fresh, asparagus gets woodier and the salad loses its sparkle.

⅓ cup dry bread crumbs, such as panko

½ cup chopped walnuts, preferably black walnuts

½ cup grated Parmigiano-Reggiano cheese

1 teaspoon grated lemon zest

¼ cup chopped fresh mint leaves

Salt and freshly ground pepper

1 pound asparagus, trimmed

1½ cups cooked, drained runner beans, such as Rancho Gordo Ayocote Morado, Ayocote Negro, or Scarlet Runner

¼ cup fresh lemon juice, plus more if needed

3 tablespoons extra-virgin olive oil, plus more if needed

MAKES 2 TO 4 SERVINGS

Preheat an oven or toaster oven to 350°F.

Place the bread crumbs and walnuts on a baking sheet and toast them until the bread crumbs are golden and the walnuts are fragrant, about 10 minutes, checking them occasionally to make sure they don't burn. Remove from the oven and let cool.

In a large serving bowl, combine the bread crumbs, walnuts, cheese, lemon zest, mint, and salt and pepper to taste. Mix well.

Using a mandoline or a very sharp knife, cut the asparagus on a sharp angle into very thin slices. In another bowl, combine the asparagus with the beans, lemon juice, and olive oil. Just before serving, add the asparagus-bean mixture to the serving bowl and toss well. Check for seasoning, adding more olive oil, lemon juice, or salt as needed.

GARBANZO SALAD WITH SHAVED RED ONIONS AND FENNEL

Fennel and garbanzos, doused with lemon and good olive oil, might be the perfect summer salad. It's fresh and clean, but it's not penance. It's delicious.

You could add some salume (Italian salted and cured meat, such as prosciutto or soppressata) if you wanted, or perhaps some grilled shrimp, but even on its own, this simple salad hits the spot.

Remember to slice the fennel bulbs as thin as you can, preferably with a mandoline. Some people have an aversion to fennel, especially fresh, raw fennel, but using a mandoline or even a potato peeler to make super thin slices makes for a wonderful crunch with just a hint of anise flavor. The more you use it, the more you are likely to appreciate its charms. Start with a little and increase as desired.

2 medium fennel bulbs

2 cups cooked, drained garbanzo beans or Rancho Gordo Black Garbanzo beans

½ red onion, thinly sliced, preferably with a mandoline

1 small bunch fresh flat-leaf parsley, chopped

3 tablespoons extra-virgin olive oil, or to taste

1 tablespoon minced preserved lemon or the zest of 1 lemon

Salt and freshly ground pepper to taste

2 tablespoons fresh lemon juice or pineapple vinegar, or to taste

MAKES 4 SERVINGS

Cut each fennel bulb in half, removing the old, tough outer skin if necessary. You can also cut out any brown spots or blemishes. Slice each half of the fennel on a thin setting of a mandoline. Alternately, slice as thinly as possible with a kitchen knife. Chop and reserve some of the fennel fronds for garnish.

In a large serving bowl, toss the fennel with the garbanzos, onion, and parsley. Add olive oil to barely coat. Add the preserved lemon and salt and pepper to taste. Squeeze in lemon juice to taste. Adjust the salt, if needed. Serve chilled or at room temperature, topped with the reserved fennel fronds.

GARBANZO SALAD WITH SPANISH CHORIZO AND RED PEPPERS

Spanish chorizo is a hard, cured sausage, unlike Mexican chorizo, which is fresh, soft, and crumbly, so make sure you're getting the right version. If you can't find it, consider a good hard salume, like pepperoni or soppressata, and maybe an extra sprinkle of pimentón (smoked paprika).

It's best to roast, peel, and seed your own red peppers, but there are some excellent jarred roasted peppers available. If using the jarred kind, rinse them before marinating in olive oil for an hour or so before adding them to the salad.

2 cups cooked, drained Rancho Gordo Garbanzo or Cecci Piccoli beans

1 cup chopped roasted red bell peppers (jarred or homemade, see page 270)

1 cup diced cured Spanish chorizo, or to taste

¼ cup minced white onion

2 to 3 tablespoons extra-virgin olive oil

1 tablespoon pineapple vinegar or other mild vinegar

Salt and freshly ground pepper

Chopped fresh flat-leaf parsley for garnish

MAKES 2 TO 4 SERVINGS

In a serving bowl, combine the garbanzos, roasted bell peppers, chorizo, and onion. Add the olive oil and pineapple vinegar. Season to taste with salt and pepper. Stir well to combine. Taste and adjust the seasonings as needed. Garnish with parsley.

BEAN SOUPS

It's interesting that so many of the hottest places in the world produce the best soups. Don't wait for cold weather to enjoy your beans in soup form. In fact, the act of making beans means you're halfway there, and bean broth is a wonderful by-product. When you make beans and you have extra liquid, always use it or save it. It's flavorful and nutritious and the exact opposite of whatever that stuff is in canned beans that needs to be rinsed and sent down the sink—except, of course, the aquafaba from canned garbanzo beans.

If you're feeling creative, sauté an onion and some garlic, pick out a few choice leftover vegetables from the fridge, and toss them together. Add a scoop full of beans, and then add bean broth and chicken or vegetable broth. Add a cheese rind, a squeeze of lemon, or even a dash of wine. You've made soup!

It's always a good idea to cut the bean broth, as bean broth alone is more often than not too dull, especially with darker beans. Chicken broth is perfect, but vegetable broth or even water works well, too. You can keep the varying textures or puree the pot in batches in a blender, or with an immersion blender right in the pot.

Starting a meal out with a soup course sends a message that you're going to some trouble. But no one has to know how easy it was to make.

SAUERKRAUT AND HEARTY WHITE BEAN SOUP

Like so many people, we're obsessed with fermenting. One of the best things to ferment is cabbage, which becomes sauerkraut with time. If you make your own sauerkraut, you may end up with an abundance, like we did. That bounty led to this dish, and even though most sauerkraut recipes seem to pair kraut with fatty meats, this soup came out vegan.

You can play with ratios of beans, kraut, and broth, but none of them should be the defining ingredient. It's not a bean soup or a sauerkraut soup; it is its own thing. If you aren't using good heirlooms like our Royal Corona beans for this recipe, the flavor won't be right. If you don't have homemade sauerkraut on hand, use a trusted brand. (There are lots of very good artisan sauerkraut makers and even some good commercial brands, if you don't want to make your own.)

5 tablespoons extra-virgin olive oil

½ medium yellow or white onion, diced

3 garlic cloves, thinly sliced

1 carrot, peeled and diced

1 celery stalk, diced

1 teaspoon dried thyme

2 cups cooked, drained Rancho Gordo Royal Corona beans or other white beans, bean broth reserved (see below)

2 to 4 cups bean broth, chicken broth, or vegetable broth, or a combination

2 cups sauerkraut, well drained

Salt and freshly ground pepper

About 2 cups Homemade Croutons (page 267)

Chopped fresh chives or dill for garnish

MAKES 4 TO 6 SERVINGS

In a large saucepan, warm 3 tablespoons of the olive oil over medium heat. Add the onion and garlic and cook, stirring, until soft and translucent, about 5 minutes. Add the carrot and celery and cook until soft, about 10 minutes. Add the thyme and cook for 1 minute.

Add the beans, broth, and sauerkraut and stir gently to combine. Simmer until the soup is thoroughly hot, about 10 minutes. Add more broth if desired. Season to taste with salt and pepper, keeping in mind that sauerkraut can be very salty.

Ladle the soup into individual bowls, garnish with the croutons and chives, and serve.

FENNEL, POTATO, AND WHITE BEAN SOUP WITH SAFFRON

Fennel, which grows wild in California, has a strong anise scent and flavor when raw that many people find to be too strong. On the other hand, cooked fennel caramelizes in the most appealing way possible, leaving just the faintest hint of anise. For raw fennel, try slicing it fine with a mandoline (watch your fingers!) or grate it. The anise flavor is there, but it's so much different than if you were to take a big bite of raw fennel.

Even though it's a sophisticated taste, once you start cooking with fennel, you'll find yourself craving it. This recipe, inspired by the restaurant Moro in London, takes full advantage of fennel's charms and ups the game with glorious bean-and-potato flavor and texture.

2 tablespoons extra-virgin olive oil, plus more for drizzling

2 tablespoons (¼ stick) unsalted butter

4 fennel bulbs (about 2 pounds total), outside layer removed, halved, and finely chopped (fronds chopped and reserved for garnish)

Salt

2 garlic cloves, thinly sliced

1 teaspoon fennel seeds

3 medium waxy potatoes (about 1 pound total), peeled and diced

4 to 6 cups bean broth, chicken broth, or vegetable broth, or a combination

1 teaspoon saffron threads, soaked in 2 tablespoons boiling water

2 cups cooked, drained white beans, such as Rancho Gordo Royal Corona or Cassoulet beans, bean broth reserved (see above)

Freshly ground pepper

MAKES 4 SERVINGS

In a large skillet, heat the olive oil and butter over medium heat. Add the fennel and a pinch of salt. Cook gently, stirring occasionally, for about 20 minutes. The fennel will start to caramelize and soften. If it begins to brown or burn, decrease the heat. Add the garlic, fennel seeds, and potatoes, stir to combine, and cook for 5 minutes.

Add the broth and saffron with its soaking water. Continue cooking until the potatoes are soft, 10 to 15 minutes. Gently fold in the beans and cook another few minutes until they are warmed through. Stir in some of the fennel fronds. Season with salt and pepper.

Ladle the soup into bowls and top each serving with the reserved fennel fronds and a drizzle of olive oil.

VARIATION: CREAMY FENNEL, POTATO, AND WHITE BEAN SOUP

If you prefer a smooth soup, this one lends itself well to pureeing. After you add the beans, use an immersion blender to blend the soup until it reaches your desired consistency. Or, ladle into a blender and, working in batches, blend and return to the pot. Heat through, add salt and pepper to taste, and stir in ¼ cup half-and-half, if you like. Garnish each serving as above.

ESCAROLE SOUP WITH GIANT WHITE BEANS AND COUNTRY HAM

Escarole, or broad-leaved endive, is another bitter vegetable that is often used raw. You can make one of the bean dips (see page 56) and use a sturdy leaf as a scoop instead of a cracker. In this soup, you'll wilt the escarole just a little so it retains some of its body and releases more flavor. To make this dish vegetarian, omit the ham.

3 tablespoons olive oil or butter, plus more if needed

8 ounces country ham, cubed

1 large leek, trimmed, rinsed, and chopped

2 garlic cloves, minced

2 tablespoons minced fresh thyme

4 to 5 cups bean broth, chicken broth, or vegetable broth, or a combination

1 head escarole, cored, leaves torn into pieces

2 cups cooked, drained large white beans, such as Rancho Gordo Royal Corona or Large White Lima beans, bean broth reserved (see above)

1 teaspoon red wine vinegar

Salt and freshly ground pepper

Freshly grated Parmesan cheese for serving

MAKES 4 TO 6 SERVINGS

In a soup pot over medium heat, warm the olive oil. Add the ham and sauté until browned around the edges, 3 to 5 minutes. Remove the ham from the pot and set aside.

Add the leek and sauté until softened, about 5 minutes, adding more olive oil if needed. Stir in the garlic and thyme.

Add the broth, increase the heat to medium-high, and bring to a boil. Add the escarole and cook, stirring, just until wilted, about 3 minutes. Add the beans and reserved ham, decrease the heat to medium-low, and simmer gently to heat the beans and ham. Taste the soup and add the red wine vinegar and salt and pepper to taste. Serve topped with Parmesan cheese.

SENATE BEAN SOUP

This is possibly Washington, D.C.'s, most famous soup. Word has it that our senators don't indulge, but rather it's mostly good citizen tourists who keep this simple dish alive. Power to the People of the Bean!

It's a very simple recipe, so it's imperative that you use the very best ingredients. It wouldn't be un-American to not follow the recipe exactly, so feel free to add even more garlic to the onion and butter, and it's likely a good pinch of thyme would pass any and all committees.

1 pound uncooked navy beans, or Rancho Gordo Yellow Eye or Alubia Blanca beans

1 pound smoked ham hocks

2 tablespoons (¼ stick) butter

½ medium yellow onion, chopped

1 celery stalk, chopped

1 garlic clove, minced

¼ cup chopped fresh flat-leaf parsley (optional)

Salt and freshly ground pepper to taste

MAKES 4 TO 6 SERVINGS

Rinse the beans and pick them over for small stones or other debris. Place the beans in a large pot and add water to cover by about 2 inches. Bring to a boil; boil for 10 to 15 minutes. Decrease the heat to low. Add the ham hocks and gently simmer, stirring occasionally, until the beans are soft and the soup is thick and creamy, 1 to 2 hours. Remove the ham hocks and set aside to cool. When cool, remove the meat from the bones, dice it, and return it to the soup.

Meanwhile, in a medium skillet over low heat, melt the butter. Add the onion, celery, garlic, and parsley (if using) and cook until the vegetables are tender, about 10 minutes. Stir the vegetable mixture into the soup. Cook for 1 more hour, adding more water if the soup is too thick. Before serving, bring to a boil and season with salt and pepper.

BREAKFAST SOUP WITH WHITE BEANS, CHICKEN STOCK, AND CHORIZO

A lot of us grew up with the understanding that cereal was breakfast, unless it was the weekend and then pancakes or waffles were in order. A savory breakfast is just as appealing, maybe more so, and even with the indulgent little bit of Mexican sausage, this soup, perfect for cold mornings, is definitely healthier than a bowl of processed wheat, sugar, and additives.

If you're so inclined, a chopped fresh chile cooked with the chorizo would be a good addition.

4 ounces good-quality fresh Mexican chorizo or soy-based chorizo

½ white onion, chopped

1 garlic clove, minced

3 to 4 cups homemade Chicken Stock (page 268) or Vegetable Stock (page 269)

2 cups cooked, drained white beans, such as Rancho Gordo Alubia Blanca beans, plus about 1 cup bean broth reserved

1 teaspoon dried Mexican oregano, preferably Rancho Gordo Oregano Indio, plus more for garnish

Salt and freshly ground pepper

2 to 4 Poached Eggs (optional; page 267)

Fresh corn tortillas, warmed

MAKES 2 TO 4 SERVINGS

In a soup pot over medium-low heat, cook the chorizo until it starts to brown and crumble. Add the onion and garlic and cook until soft and fragrant, 3 to 5 minutes. Add 3 cups of the stock, the beans, bean broth, and oregano. Increase the heat and bring to a boil. Decrease the heat and simmer for 15 to 20 minutes. Taste and season with salt and pepper. Add more stock if desired.

Transfer to bowls and sprinkle with more oregano. If desired, top with poached eggs. Serve with corn tortillas.

WHITE BEAN AND CABBAGE MINESTRONE

This is the kind of soup that your overflowing CSA vegetable subscription box has been begging for. Just as Marcella Hazan taught us in her seminal cookbook, *Essentials of Classic Italian Cooking*, it's about using what's on hand, and minestrone soup and beans go together perfectly. We love using the beans we named after Marcella herself. This recipe includes cabbage and potatoes, so it's substantial and comforting.

⅓ cup olive oil

2 tablespoons (¼ stick) butter

1 yellow onion, thinly sliced

2 carrots, peeled and diced

3 celery stalks, diced

2 garlic cloves, minced

2 medium waxy potatoes, such as Yukon gold, peeled and diced

2 to 3 cups thinly shredded savoy cabbage, green cabbage, or Tuscan kale

2 zucchini (about 8 ounces), diced

½ cup trimmed and chopped green beans

4 cups vegetable or beef broth

1 to 2 cups bean broth or water

½ cup canned whole tomatoes, preferably San Marzano

Parmesan rind

3 large basil leaves

Salt to taste

1½ cups cooked, drained white cannellini beans, such as Rancho Gordo Marcella beans, bean broth reserved (see above)

½ cup grated Parmesan cheese

Pepper to taste

MAKES 4 TO 6 SERVINGS

In a large stockpot over medium-low heat, warm the olive oil and butter. Add the onion and cook until it softens and becomes pale gold, about 10 minutes.

Add the carrots and celery and cook for 2 to 3 minutes. Add the garlic and potatoes and cook for 2 to 3 minutes. Stir in the cabbage and cook for 5 minutes. Add the zucchini and green beans and cook for 2 to 3 minutes.

Add the vegetable broth, 1 cup of the bean broth, the tomatoes, cheese rind, and basil. Salt very lightly. Stir thoroughly, increase the heat, and bring to a boil. Cover the pot, decrease the heat, and simmer for about 2½ hours, stirred occasionally, until the cabbage is silky and the zucchini is partially disintegrated. Add more bean broth if needed.

Stir in the beans and cook for 30 minutes. Just before serving, remove the cheese rind. Swirl in the grated cheese and season with salt and pepper.

VARIATION: SPRING MINESTRONE

For a "green" spring minestrone, omit the tomatoes, zucchini, and green beans. Add ½ cup diced asparagus and ½ cup fresh peas when you add the beans.

POGGIO ETRUSCO'S CLASSIC TUSCAN VEGETABLE-BREAD SOUP

Pamela Sheldon Johns is the author of numerous Italian cookbooks, including a Rancho Gordo favorite, *Cucina Povera: Tuscan Peasant Cooking*. Aside from being an accomplished author and cook, she runs an agriturismo called Poggio Etrusco, near Montepulciano in Italy. She shared her recipe for ribollita, a traditional Tuscan recipe that reflects the cucina povera, when survival was often dependent on making the most of scarce ingredients.

She says: "The evolution of the 'true' ribollita starts with leftover soup layered in a baking dish with sliced dry, stale bread (pane raffermo) and reheated in the oven for the next meal (*ribollita* literally means 'reboiled'). This repurposing is known as zuppa di pane (bread soup). On subsequent days, the true ribollita is created when a scoop of the leftover zuppa di pane is pan-fried with a small amount of extra-virgin olive oil to form a crusty exterior while the interior remains soft."

3 tablespoons extra-virgin olive oil, plus more for drizzling

1 onion, finely chopped

2 carrots, peeled and finely chopped

1 celery stalk, finely chopped

One 14-ounce can peeled Italian tomatoes and their liquid

8 cups vegetable broth

2 potatoes, peeled and cubed

3 zucchini, coarsely chopped

2 cups shredded cavolo nero (dinosaur or lacinato kale) or your choice of kale

1 cup shredded assorted leafy greens (such as Swiss chard, nettles, or spinach)

Preheat the oven to 375°F.

In a large soup pot, heat the olive oil over medium heat. Add the chopped onion, carrots, and celery and sauté for 4 to 5 minutes, or until the onion is golden. Add the tomatoes, smashing them and stirring to scrape up the browned bits from the bottom of the pot. Add the vegetable broth and increase the heat to medium-high. Add the potatoes and zucchini. Cook for 10 minutes, then add the cavolo nero and leafy greens.

Decrease the temperature to a simmer and cook for 20 minutes. Add the beans, bean broth, and herbs. Simmer for 10 minutes to heat the beans through. Season to taste with salt and pepper.

Ladle a juicy amount of the soup into your casserole dish, covering the bottom, and top with a layer of the bread. Cover the bread with additional soup, being sure that the bread is completely covered

CONTINUED

POGGIO ETRUSCO'S CLASSIC TUSCAN
VEGETABLE-BREAD SOUP, CONTINUED

2 cups cooked cannellini beans, such as Rancho Gordo Marcella beans, bean broth reserved

2 tablespoons fresh flat-leaf parsley, chopped

1 teaspoon fresh rosemary, chopped

1 teaspoon fresh marjoram, chopped

1 teaspoon fresh thyme, chopped

Sea salt and freshly ground pepper

½-inch-thick slices of stale bread (enough to make a single layer in a 9 by 13-inch casserole dish)

½ cup finely sliced white onion

MAKES 6 TO 8 SERVINGS

with soup and a generous amount of the liquid. Sprinkle with the sliced onion and drizzle with olive oil. Bake for 20 minutes, or until the onions are lightly browned.

Serve with a drizzle of olive oil.

RIBOLLITA
By Pamela Sheldon Johns

Tuscan bread, the fundamental ingredient of ribollita, typically has no salt. In Italy, salt was heavily taxed until the 1970s, and the price was prohibitive for many people. Because the salt in bread helps retain moisture, saltless bread dries out within a day. The old Tuscan proverb "Bread of one day, wine of one year" refers to the short shelf life of bread compared to the necessary aging of wine.

Because bread was usually baked once a week, Tuscans had to come up with ways to use leftover dry bread for the rest of the week. The traditional recipe for ribollita is actually the days-of-old housewife's way of using up small amounts of ingredients, including slices of dry bread.

SOPA TARASCA

This is a simple and classic soup from Michoacán, Mexico. There are actually two versions of Sopa Tarasca, but one is very complicated, and this one clearly has roots with the Purepecha people who are indigenous to the area.

Frying little strips of corn tortillas might seem fussy or unnecessary, but they really provide body and taste great. Don't skip them!

3 ancho chiles, seeded and stemmed, one halved and two cut into narrow strips

1 pound plum tomatoes

3 tablespoons extra-virgin olive oil

½ white onion, thinly sliced

2 garlic cloves, minced

4 cups cooked bayo or Flor de Mayo beans, or Rancho Gordo Cranberry or Pinto beans, bean broth reserved

3 to 4 cups chicken or vegetable broth

1 teaspoon Mexican oregano, preferably Rancho Gordo Oregano Indio

2 teaspoons salt, or to taste

Safflower or grapeseed oil for frying

2 day-old corn tortillas, cut into thin strips

½ cup crumbled queso fresco or other semi-hard white cheese

Sour cream or crema for serving

Fresh cilantro leaves for serving

MAKES 4 SERVINGS

Set a large, heavy skillet or comal over medium-high heat. Place the ancho halves in the skillet and cook for a few seconds per side, just enough to release the aroma. Transfer them to a small bowl, cover with boiling water, and let rehydrate for 10 minutes, then drain. Place the tomatoes in the skillet and cook, turning occasionally with tongs, until blackened and soft, 10 to 15 minutes. Remove the tomatoes from the skillet and chop. Set aside.

In the skillet over medium-high heat, warm the olive oil. Add the onion, garlic, and tomatoes and sauté until soft, about 10 minutes. Let cool slightly. In a blender, combine the vegetable mixture with the rehydrated ancho chile and blend until smooth. Transfer to a soup pot.

In the blender, puree the beans and their broth, adding some of the chicken broth if necessary to keep the blades moving. Transfer to the pot. Bring to a simmer and cook, stirring occasionally, for about 5 minutes. Add the chicken broth, oregano, and salt. Cook for 10 minutes to allow the flavors to blend. Taste and adjust the seasonings.

Meanwhile, pour the safflower oil to a depth of about ½ inch in a small, heavy skillet. Set the skillet over medium-high heat and heat until the oil is shimmering. Fry the tortilla strips, turning with tongs, until crisp and medium brown, 2 to 3 minutes. Remove to a paper towel. Fry the ancho chile strips until they puff up and emit a spicy aroma, 2 or 3 seconds. Remove quickly as they can become bitter if overcooked.

Put a little cheese, a few chile strips, and some tortilla strips in each bowl. Pour in the hot soup. Serve with sour cream and cilantro.

JEREMY FOX'S YELLOW EYE SOUP

Jeremy Fox's ubuntu was a seminal restaurant in Napa that made people rethink vegetarian cuisine. He's since authored a cookbook, *On Vegetables: Modern Recipes for the Home Kitchen*, and has opened two successful restaurants in Los Angeles.

Yellow eyes are usually cooked with pork, but this is a great example of a vegan preparation that elevates beans to be the star of the dish.

FOR THE BEANS

3 cups uncooked yellow eye or buckeye beans

1 carrot, peeled

2 celery stalks, halved

1 yellow onion, quartered

1 head garlic, halved crosswise

Stems from 1 bunch fresh Italian parsley, tied in cheesecloth

2 tablespoons salt

1 tablespoon freshly ground pepper

¼ cup extra-virgin olive oil

FOR THE SOUP

1 head garlic

2 leeks

¼ cup extra-virgin olive oil, plus more for drizzling

3 large carrots, peeled and diced

5 celery stalks, diced

1½ teaspoons red chile flakes

2 tablespoons chopped rosemary

1 cup canned whole San Marzano tomatoes, drained and chopped

Salt and freshly ground pepper

½ cup chopped fresh Italian parsley

Rustic bread, sliced

1 garlic clove, halved

MAKES 6 TO 8 SERVINGS

To make the beans: Pick the beans over and soak for 4 to 6 hours. Drain the beans and place them in a large pot. Add the carrot, celery, onion, garlic, and parsley stem sachet. Pour in 3 quarts cold water and bring to a boil, skimming off any foam that rises to the top. Decrease the heat to a gentle simmer and cook until the beans are soft and creamy but not falling apart, 30 to 90 minutes. (Start checking after 25 minutes; the fresher the beans, the shorter the cooking time.) Add the salt, pepper, and olive oil.

Remove the pot from the heat and discard the sachet and vegetables. Let the beans cool in their broth.

To make the soup: Peel and finely grate the garlic cloves, then set aside. Trim off the dark green leek tops, then halve the white and light green parts lengthwise. Rinse, then finely chop. Warm the olive oil in a large pot over medium heat. Add the grated garlic, leeks, carrots, celery, chile flakes, and rosemary. Cook, stirring occasionally, until the rawness of the vegetables is just gone, 3 to 4 minutes. Add the tomatoes and cook until slightly caramelized, about 3 minutes. Add the beans and their cooking broth and bring to a boil. Decrease the heat and simmer until the vegetables are tender, 5 to 10 minutes. Season to taste with salt and pepper.

Just before serving, add the parsley. Toast the bread slices. While still hot, rub them with the garlic halves, then tear into large pieces. Ladle the soup into bowls and top each with a few toasts, then drizzle with olive oil.

SOPA CAMPESINA

The spirit of this dish is to use easily available, simple ingredients, so chicken stock or meat wouldn't be included. The flavor of the beans comes through loud and clear, and the fried tortilla strips add a satisfying crunch.

Older tortillas seem to absorb less oil, so if yours are very fresh, try leaving them out on the kitchen counter for a few hours before frying them. Corn oil is traditional, but I use an organic safflower oil, which is more neutral and likely healthier.

1 tablespoon olive oil

½ white onion, chopped, plus minced onion for garnish

2 garlic cloves, minced

8 ounces uncooked dark heirloom beans, such as Rancho Gordo Moro, Lila, Rebosero, San Franciscano, or other dark bean, picked over and rinsed

Sea salt

1 to 3 tablespoons corn oil or organic safflower oil for frying

3 stale corn tortillas, cut into very thin strips

1 teaspoon dried Mexican oregano, preferably Rancho Gordo Oregano Indio

Chopped fresh cilantro for garnish

Quartered limes for garnish

MAKES 2 TO 4 SERVINGS

In a large pot over medium heat, warm the olive oil. Add the onion and garlic and sauté until soft, 6 to 8 minutes. Add the beans and cover with about 2 inches of water. Increase the heat to high and bring to a rapid boil for 10 to 15 minutes. Decrease the heat, partially cover the pot, and allow the beans to gently simmer. Make sure the beans are always covered by about 2 inches of liquid, adding more boiling water as needed. Once the beans begin to soften, after about 1 hour, add 2 teaspoons of salt (or to taste) and allow the beans to continue cooking until tender. Total time will be between 1½ and 3 hours. If it's taking too long, increase the heat.

While the beans are cooking, heat a thin layer of corn or safflower oil in a medium skillet over medium-high heat. Fry the tortilla strips, turning once, until golden and crisp, about 5 minutes. Transfer them to paper towels, then salt lightly.

When the beans are soft, taste the soup and add more salt, if desired. Add the oregano, crushing the leaves with your hands. Ladle into bowls and top with the tortilla strips, cilantro, and minced onion. Serve with the lime quarters.

MIDNIGHT BLACK BEAN SOUP

There was a time when black beans were considered very exotic to most Americans. As popular as they were in Cuba, Oaxaca, and Brazil, they didn't make a dent in American cuisine until the late 1970s. One of the first, and still most satisfying, dishes to become popular is black bean soup. If you have good heirloom black beans, try making this as simple as possible in order to enjoy the rich broth and the creamy beans. This soup pairs well with cornbread!

2 tablespoons olive oil

2 carrots, peeled and chopped

1 yellow or white onion, chopped

2 celery stalks, chopped

4 garlic cloves, minced

One 7-ounce can chipotle chiles in adobo, pureed in a food processor or blender

1 pound uncooked black turtle beans, such as Rancho Gordo Midnight Black or Santanero Negro Delgado beans, picked over and rinsed

1 tablespoon dried Mexican oregano, preferably Rancho Gordo Oregano Indio

1 bay leaf

8 cups water, plus more as needed

1 cup orange juice

1 cup canned diced tomatoes

1 tablespoon salt

1 teaspoon freshly ground pepper

Minced white onion for garnish (optional)

Chopped fresh cilantro for garnish (optional)

MAKES 4 TO 6 SERVINGS

In a large soup pot or Dutch oven over medium heat, warm the olive oil. Add the carrots, onion, celery, and garlic and cook, stirring, until softened but not browned, 5 to 8 minutes. Carefully add 2 teaspoons (or to taste) of the chipotle puree (reserve the remainder for another use) and stir until combined.

Add the beans, oregano, and bay leaf. Pour in the water. Stir, bring to a boil, and let boil for 10 to 15 minutes. Decrease the heat to a simmer and cook, partially covered, stirring occasionally, until the beans are just softened, 1 to 2 hours. Add up to 2 cups of hot water, as needed, to keep plenty of liquid in the pot. Stir in the orange juice, tomatoes, salt, and pepper and continue cooking until the beans are so soft that they crush easily against the back of a spoon. Remove and discard the bay leaf.

Adjust the texture to your liking. To thicken the soup, use an immersion blender or blender to puree 1 to 2 cups of the beans until smooth, then stir them back in. Continue until the desired texture is reached.

Before serving, heat the soup, then taste and adjust the seasonings. Serve in bowls garnished with minced onion and cilantro, if desired.

CALDINHO DE FEIJÃO
(BRAZILIAN BLACK BEAN SOUP)

A Brazilian friend and black bean aficionado, José Rivelino D. Santos Silva, served a bowl of this soup to us. It turns out it was his grandmother's recipe, and he was kind enough to share it with us. He says you can find many variations of this traditional dish throughout Brazil, especially in local botecos (bars). It's generally served with a bottle of Malagueta hot sauce, which is hard to find outside of Brazil. You can substitute with habanero hot sauce.

José always soaks his black beans—according to his family, it's the key to reducing flatulence. We won't argue with the wisdom of a Brazilian grandma! He also recommends discarding the soaking water—all but about 1 cup to add extra color to the soup.

1 smoked ham hock
(about 1½ pounds)

8 cups chicken or vegetable broth

1 bay leaf

1 pound uncooked black beans, picked over and rinsed

2 tablespoons olive oil

1 medium white onion, roughly chopped (a handful reserved for garnish)

4 garlic cloves, minced

Salt and freshly ground pepper

Lime wedges for serving

Malagueta hot sauce or habanero hot sauce for serving

SERVES 6 TO 8

The day before making the soup, combine the ham hock, chicken broth, and bay leaf in a large pot. Bring to a boil, then decrease to a simmer until the ham hock is cooked through, about 1 hour, skimming any foam that comes to the surface. Remove the ham hock and let cool. Refrigerate the broth and ham hock separately.

Soak the beans in cool water for 6 to 8 hours. Drain the beans, reserving 1 cup of the soaking liquid.

In a large pot, combine the beans, ham hock, 2 cups ham stock, the 1 cup reserved soaking water, and additional water to cover the beans by at least 2 inches. Bring to a boil over high heat, then decrease the heat to low and cook the beans gently until very soft, about 2 hours. Remove the ham hock and let cool, then remove and shred the meat and add it back to the pot.

In a medium saucepan over medium-low heat, warm the olive oil. Add the onion and garlic, and cook until soft and fragrant, 5 to 7 minutes, being careful not to brown them too much. Add 2 to 3 cups of cooked beans to the onion-garlic mixture and mash until combined (you can also use an immersion blender). Add salt to taste. Stir the onion-garlic-bean mixture back into the pot of beans. Mash the beans even further if you prefer a smoother consistency. Season to taste with salt and pepper. Add more liquid if needed for a soupy consistency. Serve in bowls garnished with onion, lime, and hot sauce.

TLAPEÑO SOUP
(MEXICAN CHICKPEA AND CHICKEN SOUP)

There are countless variations of Caldo Tlapeño, but most of them include garbanzo beans, chicken, and chipotle en adobo, which are smoked jalapeño peppers marinated in a rich tomato sauce. The adobo sauce is so good that many recipes suggest blending the entire can and adding all of it to the soup. However, chopped bits of chiles in the soup add to the texture and flavor, so you could chop them separately instead of blending.

Variations almost always include corn or zucchini or both. You can also try making this with a white bean, especially a large white runner bean, although this isn't traditional. To make this soup vegetarian, omit the chicken.

½ white onion, minced

2 chipotle chiles in adobo sauce, roughly chopped, with seeds, and about 1 tablespoon sauce

1 cup chopped tomatoes

2 garlic cloves, minced

1 tablespoon good-quality lard or olive oil

6 cups chicken or vegetable broth

2½ to 3 cups cooked Rancho Gordo Garbanzo beans, bean broth reserved

1 cup peeled and sliced carrots

2 small zucchini, sliced

1 cup cooked, shredded chicken

Avocado cubes for garnish

Lime wedges for serving

MAKES 4 TO 6 SERVINGS

In a blender, combine the onion, chipotle chiles and sauce, tomatoes, and garlic and blend until smooth.

In a stockpot or large saucepan, heat the lard over medium heat. Add the pureed vegetables and cook, stirring occasionally, for about 5 minutes. Pour in the chicken broth, bring just to a simmer, and simmer uncovered for about 15 minutes.

Add the garbanzos with their broth, carrots, and zucchini and simmer until the carrots and zucchini are barely cooked, about 8 minutes. Add the chicken and simmer until the vegetables are just cooked and the chicken and garbanzos are heated through.

Ladle the soup into individual bowls, garnish with avocado, and serve immediately. Pass the lime wedges at the table.

BEAN BRAISES, STEWS & OTHER STOVETOP DISHES

This chapter could also easily have been called "Main Courses," but one person's side dish is another person's mezze plate and still another's focus of the meal. This is really a tribute to the versatility of beans.

Stew isn't the prettiest word in the English language, and maybe it's time we reclaim it. It's not a soup. It's often more substantial but no less delicious. Maybe it's a vegan stew with big beans, fresh chard, and wild mushrooms; a tomato-based stew with white beans and seafood; an herby Persian lamb and bean stew; or one of our chilis—one with meat and the other without.

Chili is a dish that many people have strong feelings about. I always poke fun at Texans who insist on "no beans" in chili. It's tradition! You don't mess with that! I love chili in almost all of its forms and as much as I love beans, I do believe the heart and soul of the dish is chile with meat. As explained in *A Bowl of Red* by Frank X. Tolbert, the "original" chili was "simply bite size or coarsely ground beef or other mature meats cooked slowly and for a long time in boon companionship with the pulp of the chili peppers, crushed powder from the curly leaves of oregano, ground cumin seeds (*comino* in Spanish and sometimes so labeled), and chopped garlic." This should be our guide when making any chili. It's fine to add beans, a small amount of tomato, and onions, omit the meat, and innovate, but it's important to keep in mind the roots of the dish. This dish keeps evolving and I hope that your next pot continues the tradition of being a magnet for good friends. It's hard to be in a bad mood with a "bowl of red" in front of you and pals all around.

The best part of these stew-like dishes is that they're satisfying and comforting at any time of the year.

STAFFAN TERJE'S ROYAL CORONA, SWISS CHARD, AND MUSHROOM STEW

We asked our friends at Wine Forest Wild Foods to help us with a winter recipe that takes full advantage of wild mushrooms and big, fat white beans. Chef Staffan Terje (formerly of San Francisco's renowned Perbacco restaurant) delivered a vegetarian stew that would be hard not to love.

You can serve this as a side dish or a main course, maybe over cooked pasta or a toasted slice of levain or sourdough bread.

¼ cup extra-virgin olive oil, plus more for drizzling

1 large red onion, diced

2 large garlic cloves, smashed

1 large pack (40 grams) dried porcini mushrooms, preferably from Wine Forest Wild Foods, soaked in 1 quart lukewarm water for 20 minutes or up to 3 hours

2 to 3 florets fresh maitake mushrooms

2 tablespoons red miso

1 tablespoon chopped fresh thyme

4 to 6 cups cooked Rancho Gordo Royal Corona beans or other large white beans, bean broth reserved

1 bunch Swiss chard

Salt and freshly ground pepper

½ cup chopped fresh Italian parsley

2 tablespoons dried mushroom powder, preferably Wine Forest Mushroom Alchemy

Freshly grated Parmigiano-Reggiano cheese for serving

MAKES 4 TO 6 SERVINGS

In a large, heavy-bottomed pot over medium heat, warm the olive oil. Add the onion and garlic and cook until lightly browned, 5 to 10 minutes.

Reserving the soaking liquid, remove the porcini mushrooms and chop them into ½-inch pieces. Add to the pot and stir.

Gently break the maitake mushrooms into wedges and add to the pot. Stir gently and cook for about 5 minutes.

Strain the porcini-soaking water through a fine-mesh strainer or coffee filter. Do this slowly, as any sand particles will settle on the bottom of the bowl.

Add the miso and thyme to the pot and stir, then add the beans, bean broth, and porcini-soaking liquid. Add more water if necessary to cover the contents of the pot. Bring to a slow boil, then decrease the heat to a simmer.

Wash the chard and cut out the white stems. Cut the green leaves into 1-inch pieces, then slice the chard stems into 1-inch pieces. Add the chard leaves and stems to the pot and simmer until softened, about 30 minutes. Season with salt and pepper.

Add the parsley, then stir in the mushroom powder. At this point, the beans should barely be covered with liquid, which should be rich and nicely coat a spoon. Taste and adjust the seasonings.

Serve in bowls with Parmigiano-Reggiano and a drizzle of olive oil.

ROYAL CORONA BEANS IN A CREAMY TOMATO SAUCE

A rich tomato sauce provides an excellent spa treatment for white beans. This isn't your everyday tomato sauce from a jar. A homemade sauce, even with canned whole peeled tomatoes when the fresh ones are out of season, is a remarkable thing. Cooking the tomatoes brings out more of their natural lycopene (a powerful antioxidant), and while that sounds very impressive, the bigger thrill is the flavor.

In this recipe, the lily is gilded with the addition of heavy cream (or thick yogurt if you are not the glutton we'd hoped for). You could toss with pasta or serve with toasted bread for a more filling meal.

2 tablespoons olive oil

½ yellow onion, chopped

1 carrot, peeled and finely chopped

1 celery stalk, finely chopped

2 garlic cloves, minced

1 teaspoon salt, plus more to taste

One 28-ounce can whole peeled Roma tomatoes, roughly chopped and juice reserved

½ to 1 cup chicken or vegetable broth, or bean broth

½ cup dry white wine

¼ cup heavy cream or plain yogurt

3 cups cooked, drained large white beans, such as Rancho Gordo Royal Corona or Ayocote Blanco beans, bean broth reserved (see above)

Chopped fresh basil for garnish

Extra-virgin olive oil for finishing

MAKES 2 MAIN DISH SERVINGS OR
4 SIDE DISH SERVINGS

In a large skillet over medium heat, warm the olive oil. Add the onion, carrot, celery, and garlic and sauté until soft, 8 to 10 minutes. Add the salt and stir. Add the tomatoes and their juice and cook for 10 minutes. Stir in ½ cup of the broth and the wine. Cook until the liquid reduces a bit, about 10 minutes. Turn off the heat and let the sauce cool to room temperature. Stir in the cream. Add ¼ to ½ cup more broth to loosen the sauce, if needed. Stir in the beans. Turn the heat to medium-low and gently cook for 5 to 10 minutes, or until the sauce and beans are warmed through. Check for seasoning and add more salt if necessary.

Divide among bowls, sprinkle basil over the top, and finish with a drizzle of extra-virgin olive oil.

BACALAO À LA MEXICANA

Many countries have a version of salt cod in a tomato sauce with olives and capers. It's a classic dish for good reason. The Mexican version, often referred to as "à la Veracruzana," is a little different because of the chiles and the option of raisins and nuts. It's a perfect dish for the holidays. You'll want to soak your salt cod for 24 hours in advance to remove some of the saltiness.

1 pound salt cod, soaked for 24 hours with several changes of water

1 large white or yellow onion, ½ left whole and ½ finely chopped

2 tablespoons extra-virgin olive oil

4 garlic cloves, minced

5 canned plum tomatoes, roughly chopped and juice reserved

1 teaspoon dried Mexican oregano, preferably Rancho Gordo Oregano Indio

2 cups cooked, drained white beans, such as Rancho Gordo Ayocote Blanco or Alubia Blanca beans

2 roasted red bell peppers (see page 270), roughly chopped

¼ cup capers, preferably Italian capers, soaked for about 20 minutes with a few changes of water, then drained

½ cup green olives, such as Castelvetrano, pitted

Salt to taste

3 pickled jalapeños, chopped

1 small bunch fresh flat-leaf parsley, chopped

MAKES 4 TO 6 SERVINGS

In a large saucepan, barely cover the cod with water. Add the half onion and poach over medium-low heat for about 20 minutes, until cooked through. Set aside and allow to cool. Remove and discard the onion.

In a large pot, warm the olive oil over medium-low heat. Add the chopped onion and garlic and sauté until the onion is translucent, about 15 minutes. Add the tomatoes with their juice and the oregano and simmer for 10 minutes.

Remove the cod from the saucepan, reserving the poaching water. Shred the cod with your hands into small, bite-size pieces.

Add the beans, peppers, capers, and olives to the tomato sauce. Stir gently, carefully add the fish, and simmer for 10 minutes. The dish should be like a thick soup with some broth. If it seems too dry, add a little of the reserved poaching water from the cod. Taste and add salt, if desired. Divide among bowls and garnish with pickled jalapeños and parsley.

EGGS AND BEANS IN PURGATORY

Eggs in Purgatory is a classic dish. The red sauce, hot and lava-like and spiked with red pepper flakes, must be the inspiration for the name. It's an easy skillet dish and can be made more substantial with the nontraditional addition of mild or white beans. You can leave out the eggs, but we love how they make this a super-hearty meal.

The Italians have a small white bean called Purgatorio, favored by Italian food expert Judy Witts Francini, who teaches in Tuscany, the heart of bean country in Italy.

2 tablespoons extra-virgin olive oil, plus more for drizzling

3 garlic cloves, thinly sliced

2 anchovy fillets, minced (optional)

1 tablespoon capers, drained

½ teaspoon red pepper flakes, or to taste

½ yellow onion, chopped

One 28-ounce can whole tomatoes, roughly chopped and juice reserved

1½ cups cooked, drained Purgatorio beans or small white beans, such as Rancho Gordo Alubia Blanca or Marcella

Salt and freshly ground pepper to taste

1 tablespoon unsalted butter

4 eggs

¼ cup grated Parmesan cheese

4 to 8 slices crusty bread for serving

Small handful chopped fresh oregano, basil, or parsley for garnish

MAKES 4 SERVINGS

In a large skillet with a lid, heat the olive oil over medium heat. Add the garlic, anchovies (if using), capers, and red pepper flakes and cook just until the garlic turns golden brown at the edges, about 1 minute.

Stir in the onion, tomatoes with their juice, beans, and salt and pepper. Decrease the heat to medium-low and simmer, stirring often, until the tomatoes thicken into a sauce, about 15 minutes. Stir in the butter. Taste and add more salt and/or red pepper flakes (if desired). Make a small indentation in the sauce for each egg, and carefully crack them in. Sprinkle with the Parmesan. Partially cover the pan and cook until the eggs are set to your liking, 5 to 7 minutes for somewhat loose yolks.

Toast the bread in a toaster or under the broiler. Drizzle with olive oil and sprinkle with salt.

To serve, sprinkle with oregano, then spoon onto plates or into shallow bowls. Serve with the toast and pass red pepper flakes at the table.

BEANS À LA VERACRUZANA WITH OLIVES, TOMATOES, AND CAPERS

In Mexico, Veracruz is rightly considered one of the country's culinary hot spots. Since it's located on the coast, seafood is naturally a huge component of the cuisine, and Huachinango à la Veracruzana is one of the most famous dishes. A whole fresh snapper is smothered in a tomato, caper, chile, and olive sauce and baked to perfection. This method works with snapper fillets and even other kinds of fish. It dawned on us that big white beans could replace the fish, and after some experimentation, we were right. If you have a few potatoes lying around, consider boiling them, cutting them into bite-size chunks, and adding them as well.

3 tablespoons extra-virgin olive oil

1 small white onion, chopped

4 garlic cloves, minced

1 serrano or jalapeño chile, seeded and minced

1½ cups canned crushed tomatoes, juice reserved, or 5 medium tomatoes, chopped

2 bay leaves

1 teaspoon dried Mexican oregano, or 2 teaspoons fresh oregano leaves

2 sprigs thyme

½ cup halved green olives

¼ cup capers, drained

½ to 1 cup chicken or vegetable broth, or bean broth

Salt and freshly ground pepper

2½ cups cooked, drained large white heirloom beans, such as Rancho Gordo Royal Corona or Large White Lima beans, bean broth reserved (see above)

2 to 3 small potatoes, boiled and cut into 1-inch pieces (optional)

Chopped fresh parsley for garnish

Cooked white rice (optional)

MAKES 4 SERVINGS

In a medium pan, heat 2 tablespoons of the olive oil over medium-high heat. Add the onion, garlic, and chile and cook until the onion is translucent, about 5 minutes. Add the tomatoes with their juice, bay leaves, oregano, and thyme and bring to a boil. Decrease the heat to low and simmer until the liquid has reduced, about 15 minutes.

Stir in the olives, capers, and ½ cup of broth. Cook until the flavors combine, about 10 minutes. Season with salt and pepper to taste.

Once the sauce is thick and flavorful, gently stir in the beans and potatoes (if using). Add more broth if needed to loosen the sauce a bit. Cook until the beans are heated through, about 5 minutes. Remove and discard the bay leaves. Transfer to a serving dish, drizzle with the remaining 1 tablespoon olive oil, and sprinkle with parsley.

Serve over white rice (if desired).

ALUBIA BLANCAS WITH CLAMS AND SPANISH CHORIZO

White beans and seafood may not seem like an ideal pair, but the mild beans in this recipe take on a lot of flavor from the clams. You can throw in other types of seafood here too—it's easy to improvise.

Spanish chorizo is much different from Mexican-style chorizo. Mexican chorizo (and longaniza) is made with ground pork, chiles, and spices and then put into casing. Spanish chorizo is cured and aged with a completely different texture, and in this case, it's a nice contrast to the creamy beans.

4 cups cooked white beans, such as Rancho Gordo Alubia Blanca or Caballero beans, bean broth reserved

¼ cup extra-virgin olive oil

½ white onion, chopped

2 garlic cloves, chopped

1 teaspoon salt, or to taste

½ cup finely chopped Spanish-style cured chorizo

2 plum tomatoes, chopped

½ cup dry white wine

2 pounds small clams, scrubbed well

Chopped fresh parsley for garnish

Country-style bread and butter for serving

MAKES 4 TO 6 SERVINGS

In a large pot, heat the beans in their broth over medium-low heat.

In a very large lidded saucepan, warm the olive oil over medium-low heat. Add the onion, garlic, and salt and cook until soft, about 5 minutes. Add the chorizo and cook gently until some of the fat has rendered, about 5 minutes. Add the tomatoes and wine and cook to allow the flavors to mingle, 5 to 6 minutes. Increase the heat to medium and add the clams. Cover and cook for about 5 minutes, shaking the pan occasionally.

Uncover the pan and cook until all of the clams open, another few minutes. Remove the pan from the heat, then remove and discard any clams that failed to open.

Add the clam mixture to the bean pot and stir very gently until well mixed. Simmer for a few minutes to allow the flavors to mingle but not get murky.

Ladle into large, shallow bowls and sprinkle with parsley. Set out a large bowl for discarded shells and encourage your guests to eat the clams with their fingers. Pass plenty of good, hearty bread and rich, creamy butter at the table.

HEARTY SEAFOOD STEW

This is a favorite for a crowd. You can make the stew a day or two ahead, up to the point of adding the fish and shrimp. Simply reheat the pot the next day and, once simmering, add the seafood. If good shrimp are not available, use clams, scallops, or whatever looks good. Or just use fish only. There is a lot of room for improvisation.

¼ cup olive oil

1 yellow onion, thinly sliced into half-moons

2 celery stalks, thinly sliced

Salt

2 garlic cloves, peeled and smashed

1 teaspoon pure New Mexican red chile powder

One 28-ounce can whole peeled tomatoes

1 roasted red pepper, jarred or homemade (see page 270), chopped

2 cups Seafood Stock (page 268) or water

2 cups cooked, drained light beans, such as Rancho Gordo Mayocoba, or white beans, such as alubia blanca

1½ pounds halibut or another sturdy white fish, cut into 1- to 2-inch cubes

1 pound shrimp, peeled and deveined

½ teaspoon red pepper flakes, or to taste

1 bunch fresh flat-leaf parsley, roughly chopped

4 to 6 thick slices stale (or toasted) rustic bread

Lemon wedges for serving

MAKES 4 TO 6 SERVINGS

In a large pot over low heat, warm the olive oil. Add the onion, celery, and a pinch of salt. Cook, stirring occasionally, until the vegetables are soft but the onion hasn't browned, about 20 minutes. Add the garlic and chile powder and cook, stirring, for 1 minute.

Empty the can of tomatoes into a bowl and break them up into small pieces with your hands. Add the tomatoes, roasted red pepper, and stock to the pot. Gently simmer, stirring occasionally, for 30 to 40 minutes.

Add the beans. Check for seasoning and add salt to taste. Bring the pot back to a simmer and add the fish, shrimp, and red pepper flakes. Cook until the seafood is done, 2 to 5 minutes. Check again for seasoning. Remove the pot from the heat and stir in the parsley.

Place a piece of bread in the bottom of each bowl. Carefully ladle the stew over the bread. Serve with lemon wedges.

SAUTÉED ITALIAN CHARD WITH BEANS, CORN STOCK, AND CRUSHED NUTS

A big bowl of sautéed greens and heirloom beans is so simple but can be a revelation. Any hearty green, like chard, kale, or spinach, would work. One lazy Sunday, something possessed me to add a handful of dust from the bottom of a bowl of mixed nuts. It was terrific. Who knew?

1 bunch chard

¼ cup extra-virgin olive oil

½ white onion, diced

2 large garlic cloves, smashed

1 jalapeño chile, minced

Salt and freshly ground pepper to taste

2 cups cooked, drained Rancho Gordo King City Pink, Santa Maria Pinquito, or Snowcap beans, or other mild heirloom beans, plus about 1 cup bean broth reserved

2 cups homemade Corn Stock (page 269)

Handful of finely chopped nuts (or you can use the dust from the bottom of a bowl of mixed nuts!)

Squeeze of fresh lemon juice (optional)

MAKES 4 TO 6 SERVINGS

Wash the chard and cut out the stems. Cut the green leaves into 1-inch pieces, then slice the chard stems into 1-inch pieces.

In a large, heavy-bottomed pot over medium heat, warm the olive oil. Add the onion, garlic, and jalapeño and cook until lightly browned, 5 to 10 minutes. Add the chard leaves and stems to the pot and cook until softened, about 30 minutes. Season with salt and pepper. Add the beans, their broth, and the corn stock and bring to a simmer. Cook until the chard is done to your liking. Taste and adjust seasonings.

Finish with a dusting of finely chopped nuts and a squeeze of lemon (if desired).

CARNE EN SU JUGO

This is one of those dishes where the simple list of ingredients seems modest, but it's not until you make it that you realize it's a winner. It's a popular dish in the western Mexican state of Jalisco, but it doesn't seem to have traveled much farther.

Carne en su Jugo is somewhere between a soup and a stew. It's often served with boiled potatoes and refried beans on the side. It's the perfect kind of one-pot wonder that feeds a gang of friends on a Sunday evening.

4 ounces tomatillos, husks removed

2 serrano chiles, stemmed, seeded, and chopped

1 jalapeño chile, stemmed, seeded, and chopped

4 ounces lean, thin-sliced bacon, finely chopped

1 pound lean beef, such as sirloin tip or top round, thinly sliced and then chopped

4 garlic cloves, minced

3 to 4 cups beef broth

Salt and freshly ground pepper

2 cups cooked, drained Mayocoba or pinto beans

½ cup cilantro, chopped

Grilled whole green onions, minced chiles (serrano or jalapeño), quartered limes, and tortillas, for serving on the side

MAKES 4 TO 6 SERVINGS

Over high heat, bring a large pot of water to a boil. Add the tomatillos and boil until soft, 8 to 10 minutes. Drain the tomatillos, reserving the water. In a blender, puree the tomatillos with the serrano and jalapeño chiles, adding enough of the reserved cooking water to make a smooth puree. Set aside.

In a large skillet over medium-low heat, slowly cook the bacon until cooked through and the fat is rendered. Using a slotted spoon, transfer the bacon to paper towels to drain. Set aside.

Add the beef and garlic to the bacon fat. Cook, stirring frequently, for about 2 minutes.

Transfer the beef mixture to a large, heavy-bottomed pot and place over high heat. Add the tomatillo puree, 3 cups of the broth, and salt and pepper to taste (keeping in mind the salt from the bacon). Bring to a boil, then decrease the heat to medium-low and simmer for 20 minutes, adding more broth if needed. Taste and adjust the seasoning as desired.

In a small saucepan over medium heat, warm the beans.

Divide the warmed beans among wide bowls. Ladle the meat with its broth into the bowls. Sprinkle with the bacon and cilantro. Place green onions along the side of the bowls, and pass minced chiles, limes, and tortillas at the table.

SOUTHERN PINTOS
AND CORNBREAD

So many of us assume that pintos are the most popular bean in Mexico. The reality is that Mexican bean-eating is very regional. You might encounter pintos in the north, but in Oaxaca you're more than likely to eat black beans and, occasionally, runner beans (ayocote). In Guadalajara you're probably enjoying Mayocobas (also known as Peruanos), and next door in Michoacán, the beans are likely to be Flor de Mayo or Flor de Junio. So what explains the popularity of pintos in the United States? The South! Southerners love their pintos, and for many, a bowl of pinto beans and cornbread might be considered heaven, and they may not be wrong.

1 pound uncooked pinto beans, picked over and rinsed

1 ham hock (about 1 to 1½ pounds)

1 bay leaf

½ white or yellow onion, chopped

Freshly ground pepper

Salt, if needed

Cornbread for serving (see page 264 or 265)

MAKES 4 TO 6 SERVINGS

Place the beans in a large, heavy-bottomed pot along with the ham hock, bay leaf, onion, and water to cover by 2 inches. Bring to a boil over high heat and boil for 10 to 15 minutes. Decrease the heat and simmer, partially covered, stirring occasionally and adding water if the level gets too low, until the beans are very tender, 45 to 90 minutes. They should be slightly soupy.

Remove and discard the bay leaf.

Remove the ham hock and let it cool slightly. Cut the meat from the bone (or use two forks to shred it) and return the meat to the pot. Stir to combine.

Taste and season with pepper and salt, if needed. Serve with cornbread.

CLASSIC CHARRO BEANS

Charro is a classic Mexican dish with many variations. The common thread is bacon and some kind of fresh pepper.

In Michoacán, you might use Flor de Mayo or Flor de Junio beans, and in Guanajuato or Jalisco, there's a good chance that your charro beans are made with Mayocoba (also known as Peruano) beans. In the north, pintos are appropriate. In Mexico City, bayo or another light bean might be used. The point is that you shouldn't get too worried about the variety of bean used. Most medium-colored beans will work.

4 bacon slices

¼ pound good-quality loose Mexican chorizo or longaniza

½ white onion, chopped, plus more for garnish

1 to 2 serrano chiles, seeded and minced

2 garlic cloves, minced

1 teaspoon dried Mexican oregano, preferably Rancho Gordo Oregano Indio

½ red bell pepper, chopped

1 cup chopped whole canned tomatoes

4 to 6 cups cooked medium-bodied beans, such as Flor de Junio, pinto, or Mayocoba, bean broth reserved

½ to 1 cup chicken or vegetable broth or water, if needed

Salt to taste

Lime wedges for serving

MAKES 4 TO 6 SERVINGS

In a medium pot over medium-low heat, cook the bacon until the fat has rendered. Remove from the pot and chop into small pieces. Set aside.

Increase the heat to medium, add the chorizo to the pot, and cook, stirring, until browned, about 10 minutes. Add the onion and serrano chiles and cook until soft, 5 to 7 minutes. Stir in the garlic, oregano, bell pepper, and tomatoes and cook for 2 to 3 minutes.

Add the beans and their broth to the pot. Simmer for 15 to 20 minutes. If more liquid is needed, add chicken or vegetable broth. Charro beans are soupy! Taste and add salt if needed. Divide among bowls and top with the bacon and raw onion. Serve with lime wedges.

VARIATION: BORRACHO BEANS

Borracho beans are just charro beans with the addition of beer. *Borracho* means "drunk." A half a cup or so is delicious, but don't be heavy-handed or you'll have a very yeasty dish. I prefer a darker Mexican-style beer like Negra Modelo. Add the beer along with the beans and their broth, then let simmer for 15 to 20 minutes.

VARIATION: VEGETARIAN CHARRO BEANS

Omit the bacon and chorizo and bulk up the garnishes, adding chopped tomatoes, cubed avocado, sautéed mushrooms, poblano strips (see page 245), crumbled cheese, and/or chopped fresh cilantro.

SOUTHWESTERN CHILI CON CARNE

Chili is one of America's favorite dishes. It's a marriage of the new and old worlds, and it acknowledges our huge debt to our neighbors south of the border.

Each cook can do little things to make it his or her own, but the heart and soul of the dish is chile with meat, as the name makes clear. As with most good food, if you use the right ingredients, you need to stay out of the way and let them shine. We love beans in a chili, but in particular, we love the bean broth, which can make the chili downright velvety.

¼ cup olive oil

2 pounds chuck roast, cut into ½- to 1-inch cubes

2 white onions, chopped, plus more for garnish

4 to 6 cloves garlic, minced

¼ cup pure New Mexican red chile powder, plus more for garnish

1 tablespoon dried Mexican oregano, preferably Rancho Gordo Oregano Indio

1 teaspoon ground cumin

3 cups water

One 12-ounce bottle Negra Modelo or other dark beer

3 cups cooked, drained hearty heirloom beans, such as Rancho Gordo Vaquero, Domingo Rojo, or Good Mother Stallard beans, plus about 1 cup bean broth reserved

Salt to taste

1 tablespoon masa harina (optional)

Chopped cilantro for garnishing (optional)

Hot flour tortillas, buttermilk biscuits, or your favorite cornbread for serving

MAKES 4 SERVINGS

In a stockpot over medium heat, warm the olive oil. Working in batches, sear the beef cubes on all sides, removing them as they brown. Set the beef aside.

Decrease the heat and add the onions and garlic to the pot. Cook, stirring frequently, until the onions are soft. Add the chile powder, oregano, and cumin and cook, stirring, until fragrant. Slowly pour in the water and beer and bring to a boil.

Decrease the heat to low and return the beef cubes to the pot. Allow to simmer gently for about 2 hours, stirring occasionally.

Add the beans and their broth, and salt to taste. Cook for about 10 minutes, until the beans are heated through. The texture should be somewhat soupy, but if the liquid is too thin, dissolve the masa harina in about ½ cup of water. Stir well to avoid any lumps. Slowly add the liquid to the chili. Cook on low for about 15 minutes.

Ladle the soup into bowls and garnish with onion, cilantro, and chile powder (if desired). Serve with hot flour tortillas, buttermilk biscuits, or cornbread.

BEANS TOPPED WITH NOPALES, FIERY SALSA, AND ONION

Nopales are the vegetable paddles of the prickly pear cactus (*Opuntia ficus-indica*) that have been eaten for centuries by Mesoamerican cultures. The red, green, and yellow fruits ("tunas" in Mexico) have been adopted in other countries, especially in Italy, but the paddles are more common in Mexico. It's a shame because they are delicious, sustainable, and incredibly healthy. In Mexico, when someone has an inclination toward diabetes, the first thing advised is nopales. Similarly, tunas are recommended for people with high blood pressure. It's an amazing plant that survives in all kinds of environments, even snow, as long as it is accommodated with very well-drained soil.

The best paddles for eating are floppy but not droopy; at this stage, many of the painful glochids (the prickly part of prickly pear) have yet to form. Once cut, the sides of the paddles are trimmed and then the glochids are removed with a sharp knife, first in one direction, then another. It's hard at first, but you get the hang of it. If you do find the glochids have attached to your fingers, and they will, try removing them with tape and then tweezers.

2 nopales (cactus paddles), cleaned (see headnote)

¼ white onion, chopped, plus more for serving

3 to 4 cups cooked heirloom beans, such as Rancho Gordo Ayocote Morado, Ayocote Negro, or Buckeye, or other heirloom beans, such as tepary or Zuni Gold, bean broth reserved

Salt and pepper to taste

Lime juice to taste

De Árbol Chile Salsa (page 260) or your favorite salsa

Warm corn tortillas or cornbread for serving (see page 264 or 265)

MAKES 4 SERVINGS

Cut the cleaned nopales into ½-inch cubes. In a large saucepan over medium heat, combine the nopales with the onion, plus enough water to cover them by 1 inch. Simmer until the nopales are cooked but still al dente, about 10 minutes. Strain and reserve the vegetables, discarding the water.

In a small saucepan, warm the beans and their broth, tasting the broth for seasoning and adding salt, pepper, and a squeeze of lime juice if needed. Divide the beans and broth among 4 bowls. Top with the cooked nopales, chopped raw onion, and a spoonful of salsa over each bowl. Serve with warm corn tortillas or cornbread.

RANCHO GORDO CHILI SIN CARNE

The chili debate is one of my favorites. Texans can be stubborn, and most will tell you that beans have no business in chili con carne. You can easily shrug and ignore them, doing what pleases you. However, bean broth adds something special to chili, even if you have few or no beans.

The Texas aversion to beans in chili is understandable when you have a traditional Texas chili and then compare it to what is basically a vegetable stew with a few jalapeños in it. A hot vegetable stew is not chili, even if you make it spicy. A much bigger issue than beans in the chili debate is tomatoes. They are sweet, juicy, and acidic, but they really are wrong for this dish. Try making chili with dried chiles and no tomatoes, and see if you don't agree. We've substituted meat in this version with big, beefy runner beans. A stubborn Texan isn't likely to budge, but serve it with cornbread and enjoy yourself.

¼ cup olive oil

2 garlic cloves, minced

½ white onion, chopped

2 tablespoons pure New Mexican red chile powder

1 teaspoon ground cumin

1 teaspoon dried Mexican oregano, preferably Rancho Gordo Oregano Indio

2 cups vegetable broth

4 cups cooked, drained hearty heirloom beans, such as Rancho Gordo Ayocote Negro, Ayocote Morado, Scarlet Runner, or Domingo Rojo, plus about 1 cup of bean broth reserved

Salt to taste

Sugar (optional)

4 small zucchini (or 2 large), sliced into rounds or on a bias

Corn kernels, from 3 ears of corn

Lime wedges and/or crème fraîche for serving (optional)

MAKES 6 TO 8 SERVINGS

In a large pot, such as an enameled cast-iron Dutch oven, heat the olive oil over medium-low heat until it ripples. Add the garlic and onion and sauté until fragrant, about 5 minutes. Add the chile powder, cumin, and oregano and cook, stirring constantly, for 3 minutes. You should have a dense paste.

Very slowly, mix in the vegetable broth, stirring constantly until well blended. Gently add the beans and their broth and stir to combine. Cook for about 20 minutes, stirring occasionally. Taste and add salt if needed. If the broth is overly bitter, add sugar, 1 teaspoon at a time, until the flavor is correct.

Continue simmering, stirring occasionally, until the chili has started to thicken and there is no grainy texture from the chile powder.

Add the zucchini and corn and cook for 15 minutes.

Serve with lime wedges and a bowl of crème fraîche (if desired).

HEIDI SWANSON'S CHRISTMAS LIMA STEW

Cookbook author and chef Heidi Swanson has been a constant supporter of beans. She hunts for them at farmers' markets, in her travels around the world, and even at the grocery store. Her creativity with beans seems endless; she is a real friend of the bean. She wrote this recipe with Christmas limas in mind, but any lima or even Royal Corona beans would substitute. Heidi's recipe was inspired by and adapted from Hassan's Celery and White Bean Soup with Tomato and Caraway in *Moro East* by Sam and Sam Clark.

1 cup extra-virgin olive oil

2 large heads celery, preferably with leaves, trimmed then sliced into ¾-inch chunks (leaves reserved for making celery salt)

3 bunches green onions or 12 spring onions if in season, green parts included, sliced into ⅓-inch rounds

8 garlic cloves, very thinly sliced

Scant 2 teaspoons caraway seeds, lightly crushed

Fine sea salt

One 28-ounce can whole plum tomatoes, drained, rinsed, cored, and roughly chopped

2 to 4 teaspoons homemade Celery Salt (recipe follows) or store-bought

4 to 6 cups cooked Rancho Gordo Christmas Lima beans, bean broth reserved

Oily black olives, pitted and roughly chopped, for garnish

1 lemon, cut into eighths

MAKES 8 SERVINGS

Heat ¾ cup of the olive oil in a large pot over medium-high heat. Add the celery and stir until coated with oil. Cook for 10 minutes, stirring often. Add two-thirds of the green onions, the garlic, caraway seeds, and a couple big pinches of salt. Cook for 10 to 15 minutes, or until the vegetables soften and begin to caramelize a bit.

Add the tomatoes and 2 teaspoons of the celery salt and cook for another few minutes. Add the beans along with 5½ cups of liquid (ideally 2 cups bean broth plus 3½ cups water) and the remaining ¼ cup olive oil.

Bring to a simmer, taste, and season with more salt or celery salt if needed. Ladle the stew into bowls and top with a spoonful of chopped olives and a squeeze of lemon. Garnish with the remaining green onions.

CELERY SALT

Celery leaves (reserved from
Heidi Swanson's Christmas
Lima Stew)

Flaky salt

MAKES 1 TO 2 TABLESPOONS
(DEPENDING ON HOW MANY
CELERY LEAVES YOU HAVE)

Preheat the oven to 250°F.

Make sure the leaves are as dry as possible if you've recently washed them. (If they're damp, they'll steam rather than crisp.) Spread out the leaves on a baking sheet and bake for 15 to 25 minutes, tossing once or twice, until dried out. Alternately, you can toast them in a large skillet over low heat, tossing regularly, for about 30 minutes.

Crumble the dried celery leaves with an equal part flaky salt. Store in a spice jar or other lidded container.

KHORESH-E GHORMEH SABZI
(PERSIAN HERB, BEAN, AND LAMB STEW)

Many refer to this as Iran's national dish. The ingredient list can seem daunting if you aren't familiar with Persian cooking, but this slow-simmered, herby stew is a culinary wonder worth all the fuss. Najmieh Batmanglij shared her recipe with us, from her seminal book *Food of Life: Ancient Persian and Modern Iranian Cooking and Ceremonies.* Dried fenugreek leaves and dried Persian limes are available at Persian markets and online. Serve with hot rice such as the traditional chelow (saffron-steamed rice).

FOR THE LAMB

2 tablespoons vegetable oil, butter, or ghee

2 large yellow onions, sliced

4 garlic cloves

1½ pounds boned shoulder or leg of lamb, cut into 2-inch pieces

1 tablespoon sea salt

1 teaspoon freshly ground pepper

1 teaspoon ground turmeric

2 teaspoons ground cardamom

3 cups water

¾ cup uncooked kidney beans or Rancho Gordo Domingo Rojo beans, soaked overnight, drained, and rinsed

6 whole limoo omani (dried Persian limes), pierced

To make the lamb: In a Dutch oven, heat the vegetable oil over medium heat. Add the onions, garlic, and lamb and cook until the lamb is browned on all sides. Add the salt, pepper, turmeric, and cardamom and sauté for 1 minute.

Pour in the water. Add the beans and the whole limoo omani. Bring to a boil, decrease the heat to low, cover, and simmer for 1 hour, stirring occasionally.

To prepare the herbs: Meanwhile, in a wide skillet, heat the vegetable oil over medium heat. Add the parsley, chives, cilantro, and fenugreek and cook, stirring frequently, for about 30 to 40 minutes, until the aroma of frying herbs rises. (This stage is very important to the taste of the khoresh. Be careful not to burn the herbs.)

Add the sautéed herbs to the pot and stir. Cover and simmer for another 2 hours over low heat, stirring occasionally.

Add the lime juice and saffron mixture to the pot. Stir, cover, and cook for 30 minutes.

Check to see if the lamb and beans are tender. Taste the khoresh and add more salt or lime juice, if desired. Transfer to a deep casserole and serve hot with chelow (saffron-steamed rice). Nush-e Jan!

CONTINUED

FOR THE HERBS

¼ cup vegetable oil or olive oil

4 cups finely chopped fresh parsley, or 1⅓ cups dried (see Notes)

1 cup finely chopped fresh chives or spring onions, or ⅓ cup dried (see Notes)

1 cup finely chopped fresh cilantro, or ⅓ cup dried (see Notes)

3 tablespoons dried fenugreek leaves (see Notes), or 1 cup chopped fresh fenugreek

2 tablespoons fresh lime juice

½ teaspoon ground saffron dissolved in 2 tablespoons rose water

MAKES 6 SERVINGS

Notes: If using dried herbs, place them in a sieve, immerse in a bowl of cold water, and soak for 20 minutes. Lift up the sieve to drain before sautéing the herbs.

For this recipe you cannot substitute the fenugreek leaves with anything else. If you don't have fenugreek, don't make this recipe (and don't use more than 3 tablespoons of dried fenugreek, as it is very strong and will make the khoresh bitter).

VARIATION: VEGETARIAN KHORESH-E GHORMEH SABZI

Eliminate the meat from the recipe and increase the kidney beans to 1 cup. Proceed with the recipe.

BASQUE-STYLE BEAN AND KALE STEW

A recipe from the UK paper *The Guardian*, by Spanish chef José Pizarro, caught our eye: a traditional Basque stew using Tolosa beans, which are famous and somewhat wonderful. A runner bean like ayocote negro would be close, but not quite. We decided to try the stew with our Chiapas Black beans, and friends, it was something! We've modified the recipe to make it our own, and it's a keeper. We hope our Basque friends will like our version too.

3 tablespoons extra-virgin olive oil, plus more for finishing

1 large yellow onion, chopped

1 large leek, white and light green parts, trimmed and finely sliced

1 bay leaf

A few sprigs each fresh thyme and oregano

2 garlic cloves, finely sliced

1 teaspoon Spanish pimentón (smoked paprika)

Pinch of red pepper flakes

1 cup dry white wine

2 to 3 cups cooked, drained Negras de Tolosa, Rancho Gordo Chiapas Black beans or Black Garbanzo beans, or any other dried black beans, plus about 1 cup bean broth reserved

2 to 3 cups chicken or vegetable broth

Salt

1 small bunch Tuscan kale (cavolo nero) or curly kale, thick stalks removed and leaves shredded

¾ cup shredded smoked ham hock

2 teaspoons pineapple vinegar or sherry vinegar

Freshly ground pepper

MAKES 4 TO 6 SERVINGS

In a large pot over medium heat, warm the olive oil. Add the onion and leek and cook, stirring, until softened, about 10 minutes. Add the bay leaf, thyme, oregano, garlic, pimentón, and red pepper flakes and cook, stirring, for a few minutes more. Add the wine, increase the heat, and cook until reduced by about half.

Add the beans, bean broth, and chicken broth. Decrease the heat, season generously with salt, and simmer gently, uncovered, for 20 to 30 minutes, until the juices have reduced and thickened.

Add the kale, cover the pot, and cook for 4 to 5 minutes, just to wilt the greens. Stir in the shredded ham and pineapple vinegar and cook to heat through. Remove and discard the bay leaf. Ladle into bowls and serve with a drizzle of olive oil, a scattering of red pepper flakes (if desired), and a good grind of pepper.

VARIATION: VEGETARIAN BEAN AND KALE STEW

The pork is essential for a more traditional dish, but replacing it with ¾ cup cooked, seasoned tofu cubes would be delicious.

RANCHO MELADUCO'S PINQUITO BEANS WITH MEDJOOL DATES

You might wince at the idea of beans, dates, and bacon in one dish, but we promise you, this recipe from date producer Rancho Meladuco of California's Coachella Valley, created by Julia Heffelfinger and shared with us by Joan Smith, will be a favorite. The texture is otherworldly, and the flavors are both familiar and exciting at the same time. Please use quality ingredients or this might end up a stodgy mess.

FOR THE BEANS

1 pound uncooked Santa Maria pinquito beans

1 yellow or white onion, halved

5 large garlic cloves, smashed

2 bay leaves

FOR THE SAUCE

1 large Anaheim chile

1 pound smoked thick-cut bacon, diced

1 white onion, minced, some reserved for garnish

4 garlic cloves, minced

1 teaspoon pure New Mexican chile powder

1 teaspoon ground cumin

1 teaspoon ground mustard

2 cups tomato puree

1 cup Mexican-style lager

½ cup brewed coffee

5 Medjool dates, preferably from Rancho Meladuco, pitted and chopped

Salt and freshly ground pepper

Mexican crema for serving (optional)

MAKES 6 TO 8 SERVINGS

To make the beans: Rinse and sort the beans. If desired, soak the beans in cold water for 4 to 8 hours, then drain. Place the beans in a large pot and cover with fresh cold water by 3 inches. Add the onion, garlic, and bay leaves and bring to a boil over high heat. Boil for 10 to 15 minutes. Decrease the heat to a simmer and cook gently, uncovered, until the beans are tender, 45 minutes to 2 hours. Add hot water, as needed, to keep the beans covered.

To make the sauce: While the beans are simmering, char the Anaheim chile over a burner on the stovetop or under the broiler until completely charred. Transfer to a resealable plastic bag (or place in a bowl and cover with a plate) and let sit for 15 minutes. Once cool enough to handle, rub a paper towel over the chile to remove the skin. Finely chop the chile and discard the seeds and stem. Set aside.

In a large saucepan or Dutch oven, cook the bacon over medium heat, stirring occasionally, until it's crispy and browned, 10 to 20 minutes. Using a slotted spoon, transfer one-quarter of the bacon to a paper towel–lined plate to drain. Reserve for garnishing. Pour out some of the bacon fat, if desired.

In the same saucepan, add the onion and cook until translucent, about 5 minutes. Add the garlic and cook until fragrant, about 1 minute. Add the chile powder, cumin, and mustard and cook, stirring occasionally, until fragrant, about 1 minute. Stir in the tomato puree, lager, coffee, dates, and reserved chile. Season with salt and pepper. Bring to a boil, then decrease the heat to low and simmer, stirring occasionally, until the sauce is thickened and the dates are beginning to break down, 30 to 40 minutes.

Drain the beans, reserving 1 cup of the bean broth. Discard the onion, garlic, and bay leaves. Return the beans to the pot. Stir in the sauce and the reserved bean broth, and cook over low heat until heated through. Season with salt.

Transfer the beans to a serving bowl and garnish with the reserved bacon, white onion, and a spoonful of Mexican crema (if desired). Serve right away.

SANTA MARIA BARBECUE–STYLE PINQUITO BEANS

The classic Santa Maria barbecue menu is a tri-tip and pinquito beans. Stories exist that pinquito beans arrived in California during the Mission era, while others claim the beans arrived in California with migrant citrus workers. However they landed, they are an essential part of California cuisine, as is the tri-tip. The best of both are cooked over California oak chips in a traditional Santa Maria barbecue, but you can replicate a traditional meal without it.

1 pound uncooked Santa Maria pinquito beans, picked over and rinsed

1 bay leaf

2 to 3 bacon slices, chopped (optional)

Olive oil, as needed

1 medium yellow onion, chopped

3 garlic cloves, minced

2 teaspoons ground mustard

1 teaspoon chili powder blend or New Mexican chile powder, or to taste

1 teaspoon light brown sugar

1 cup tomato puree or diced tomatoes

1 tablespoon Worcestershire sauce

Salt and freshly ground pepper

MAKES 6 TO 8 SIDE DISH SERVINGS

Place the beans and bay leaf in a stockpot. Add water to cover the beans by about 2 inches and bring to a boil. Boil for 10 to 15 minutes. Decrease the heat to low and simmer, partially covered, until the beans are beginning to soften, about 1 hour.

Meanwhile, in a medium skillet over medium heat, cook the bacon (if using) until the fat has mostly rendered, 5 to 7 minutes. If not using bacon, warm about 2 tablespoons of olive oil. Add the onion and garlic and cook until softened, about 10 minutes. Add the mustard, chili powder, sugar, tomato puree, and Worcestershire sauce and cook for 5 minutes.

Drain the beans, returning them to the stockpot and reserving the bean broth. Remove and discard the bay leaf. Stir the onion mixture into the beans, along with about 1 cup of the bean broth. Season to taste with salt and pepper. Simmer for about 30 minutes, adding more cooking time as needed to obtain the desired consistency. Keep warm until ready to serve.

GARBANZOS WITH SAUTÉED SPINACH AND PIMENTÓN

Garbanzos con Espinacas is a classic Spanish dish that is deceptively simple. You'll want to use the best pimentón from Extremadura that you can find, and if you are so inclined, you'll find fresh spinach is worth the extra bother over frozen. Serve this dish on its own or with rice or flatbread.

2 tablespoons extra-virgin olive oil, plus more for drizzling

1 white onion, finely chopped

4 garlic cloves, minced

2 to 3 teaspoons Spanish pimentón (smoked paprika)

Salt to taste

2 cups cooked, drained Rancho Gordo Garbanzo beans, plus 1 to 2 cups bean broth reserved

3 cups thawed frozen spinach (from two 10-ounce packages), drained and squeezed dry, or 3 cups cooked spinach (3 pounds of fresh spinach will cook down to about 3 cups)

Lemon wedges for serving

MAKES 2 TO 4 SERVINGS

In a deep skillet over medium heat, warm the olive oil. Add the onion and garlic and sauté until fragrant, 2 to 3 minutes. Add the pimentón and salt and cook, stirring, until combined. Then add the garbanzo beans and 1 cup bean broth and bring to a simmer. Stir in the spinach. Cook until the spinach is heated through and the flavors have mingled. Stir in an additional cup of broth if needed.

Transfer to a serving bowl and top with a generous drizzle of olive oil and a squeeze of lemon.

CHRISTMAS LIMAS IN A GORGONZOLA CREAM SAUCE

This dish was inspired by the classic Italian Gnocchi in Gorgonzola. Christmas limas have an interesting texture, and it seems natural to pair them with a rich cheese sauce. You can try this with other blue cheeses, but Gorgonzola works best.

The amount of cream and cheese you use depends on your preference. The more cream you use, the thinner the sauce will be. The more cheese you use, the stronger the flavor will be.

1 tablespoon olive oil

½ cup cubed pancetta (about 4 ounces)

1 small white onion, chopped

2 garlic cloves, minced

1 cup half-and-half, or to taste (see headnote)

½ cup crumbled Gorgonzola or blue cheese, or to taste

4 cups cooked, drained Rancho Gordo Christmas Lima beans

Salt and freshly ground pepper to taste

Chopped fresh parsley for garnish

MAKES 4 SIDE DISH SERVINGS

In a large pan or skillet over medium-low heat, warm the olive oil. Add the pancetta, onion, and garlic and cook until the pancetta and onion begin to brown, 10 to 15 minutes. Add the half-and-half and whisk until it begins to bubble. Add the cheese and whisk until the sauce reduces and is thick enough to coat the back of a wooden spoon.

Add the beans to the sauce and let them get to know each other for a few minutes, but not too long. Season to taste with salt and pepper. Garnish with a bit of parsley.

VARIATION: MUSHROOM-GORGONZOLA CREAM SAUCE

Use 8 ounces of fresh mushrooms (wiped cleaned and roughly chopped) in place of the pancetta, and increase the olive oil to ¼ cup.

LABLABI (TUNISIAN CHICKPEA STEW)

Like most bean dishes, this North African stew has many variations depending on the region in which it's served. Sometimes half of the garbanzo beans are pureed and stirred back into the soup, other times not; the toppings can range from capers to olives to green onions to eggs.

If you've already cooked a pot of garbanzos, you have the beans but also the incredible bean broth ready to be put to work in a brothy stew like this. The rest of the ingredients should be readily available at most American supermarkets. Harissa is a North African chile sauce that's become a popular condiment in the United States. If you can't find it at your local store, you could use any chile paste or chile sauce you like, or make your own version.

Extra-virgin olive oil

1 large yellow onion, chopped

4 garlic cloves, minced

1 teaspoon ground cumin, plus more for garnish

½ teaspoon ground coriander

4 to 6 cups cooked, drained Rancho Gordo Garbanzo beans, bean broth reserved (see below)

4 to 6 cups bean broth, vegetable broth, or water (or a combination)

4 to 6 small but thick slices rustic bread

2 tablespoons fresh lemon juice

2 tablespoons harissa, homemade or store-bought, plus more for serving

¼ cup chopped green olives (optional)

Salt and freshly ground pepper

4 to 6 soft-cooked eggs, peeled and halved (optional)

⅓ cup chopped fresh flat-leaf parsley

Lemon wedges for serving

MAKES 4 TO 6 SERVINGS

In a large pot over medium-low heat, warm 2 tablespoons olive oil. Add the onion and cook, stirring occasionally, until lightly golden, about 5 minutes. Stir in the garlic and cook until fragrant, about 30 seconds. Stir in the cumin and coriander and cook until fragrant, about 1 minute. Add the garbanzo beans and broth, increase the heat to high, and bring to a boil. Decrease the heat to medium-low and simmer, uncovered, until the liquid has reduced a bit and the garbanzo beans are hot, 15 to 20 minutes. For a thicker consistency, transfer about 1 cup of garbanzo beans to a blender, puree, and return them to the pot.

Meanwhile, brush the bread slices with olive oil. Toast under a broiler until golden and crisp, 1 to 2 minutes.

Remove the pot from the heat and stir in the lemon juice, harissa, and olives (if using). Season to taste with salt and pepper.

To serve, place a slice of toasted bread in each bowl. Ladle the stew into the bowls, then drizzle with olive oil. Garnish to taste with harissa and cumin, then top each portion with two soft-cooked egg halves (if desired) and parsley. Serve with lemon wedges.

FAITH KRAMER'S CHOLENT
(JEWISH SHABBAT STEW)

Faith Kramer is a food writer and recipe developer concentrating on the foodways, history, and customs of the Jewish diaspora. She knows a great deal about the ancient dish Cholent, or Jewish Shabbat Stew, and she shared some background on it, as well as one of her own versions, which combines the traditional chickpeas, beef, potatoes, onions, and hard-cooked eggs with an array of seasonings.

She says: "Long-simmered bean, meat, and grain stews have a special place in Jewish culinary history. From early medieval times, Jews have been serving hearty, long-cooked dishes that allow them to serve a special, hot meal for lunch on the Jewish Shabbat (Sabbath). The overnight cooking technique evolved since observant Jews perform no work from Friday sunset to Saturday nightfall and actively cooking food comes under that ban."

Cholent is great to make ahead and tastes even better reheated the next day. Faith likes to serve it with pickles or pickled vegetables, challah or other bread, and a salad. She always passes some harissa or other hot sauce alongside.

1½ cups uncooked garbanzo beans, soaked for 6 to 8 hours

2½ teaspoons salt

1½ teaspoons ground pepper

1½ teaspoons paprika

2½ pounds boneless beef chuck roast or brisket, cut into 1½-inch cubes

3 tablespoons vegetable oil

2 large yellow onions, thinly sliced

12 medium garlic cloves, minced

1½ teaspoons ground cumin

1 teaspoon ground cinnamon

½ teaspoon ground turmeric

½ teaspoon crushed red pepper flakes

CONTINUED

Drain the garbanzo beans and discard the soaking liquid. Set aside.

In a large bowl, mix 2 teaspoons of the salt, 1 teaspoon of the pepper, and 1 teaspoon of the paprika. Place the beef cubes in the bowl and toss well until they're covered with the spices. Set aside.

In an 8-quart Dutch oven or large ovenproof pot with a lid, heat the vegetable oil over medium-high heat. Add the onions and cook, stirring occasionally, until soft and translucent, about 7 to 10 minutes. Add the garlic and sauté until golden, about 1 to 2 minutes. Sprinkle in the cumin, cinnamon, turmeric, red pepper flakes, and the remaining ½ teaspoon each salt, pepper, and paprika. Cook, stirring, until fragrant, about 1 minute.

4 to 6 cups vegetable or chicken broth

¾ cup uncooked whole freekeh or pearled barley, rinsed

4 medium white potatoes or sweet potatoes

4 medium carrots, peeled

3 tablespoons honey, plus more as needed

2½ tablespoons tamarind paste or concentrate (see Note)

2 tablespoons tomato paste

8 large eggs in the shell

2 tablespoons fresh lemon juice (from 1 medium lemon), or to taste

8 lemon wedges for serving

3 tablespoons chopped fresh parsley

MAKES 6 TO 8 SERVINGS

Stir in 4 cups of the broth, the garbanzos, beef (with any loose seasonings left in the bowl), and the freekeh. Bring to a simmer. Decrease the heat and simmer, covered, for 1 hour.

Preheat the oven to 250°F.

Peel and cut the potatoes into 1-inch chunks (about 3 cups). Cut the carrots into 1-inch pieces (about 2 cups). Add the potatoes, carrots, honey, tamarind paste, and tomato paste to the pot and stir well. Add additional broth as needed to keep the meat and vegetables covered. Return to a simmer. Snuggle the eggs among the ingredients on top, making sure they are covered with broth.

Cover the pot with aluminum foil and then put the lid on to create a strong seal. Place in the oven and cook for 10 to 14 hours, checking occasionally to stir and add broth or water so the pot does not dry out. Decrease the oven to 200°F if the cholent seems to be sticking or burning.

The garbanzos and freekeh should be cooked through but not mushy. The meat should be very tender. The sauce should be thick and not soupy. The eggs will be cooked through, and their shells may be cracked. Remove the eggs and peel. Stir in the lemon juice. Taste the sauce and stir in additional honey or lemon juice as desired. Add salt if needed. Serve in bowls, each serving accompanied by a cooked egg and a lemon wedge and garnished with parsley.

Note: Jarred tamarind paste or concentrate is made from the seedless pulp of the tamarind. It has a fruity, sharp, and slightly sweet taste. Do not substitute the block, dried tamarind. Tamarind is available in Indian, Middle Eastern, and other specialty stores and online.

VARIATION: SLOW COOKER

This recipe is for an 8-quart slow cooker. Adjust the quantities as needed for size. Refer to the manufacturer's instructions.

Season the beef as directed in the main recipe. Turn the slow cooker on high and let heat, covered, for 15 minutes if using a ceramic insert or 5 minutes if using a metal one. Add the vegetable oil and let heat for a few minutes. Add the onions and garlic. Let cook, stirring occasionally, until beginning to soften. Stir in the cumin, cinnamon, turmeric, red pepper flakes, and remaining ½ teaspoon each salt, pepper, and paprika. Add the broth, beef, drained garbanzos, freekeh, potatoes, carrots, honey, tamarind, tomato paste, and eggs. Decrease the heat to low. Cover and let cook for 14 to 18 hours, adding liquid as needed. If the sauce is too thin, allow to cook, uncovered, on high for the last 30 to 60 minutes. Taste and correct the seasonings as directed in the main recipe.

VARIATION: SLOW-COOKING ON STOVETOP

The stew can be cooked on the stovetop on as low a heat as possible with the pot set on a metal flame tamer or blech (a thin sheet of metal or an old baking sheet will work). Cover as above. Cook for 10 to 14 hours, checking occasionally to stir and add broth if needed. If the pot will be left unattended overnight, be sure there is sufficient liquid in the pot to prevent burning and drying out.

SPANISH FABADA
(PORK AND BEAN STEW)

Unless you're cooking this in Spain, the real challenge will be finding the right cuts of meat and other ingredients. Pancetta, Spanish chorizo, and pimentón are easy enough to find, but morcilla, an incredibly delicious blood sausage, might be a challenge. There is nothing quite like it, but even without blood sausage, you'll still have a delicious pot. Taylor Boetticher of the Fatted Calf and co-author of *In the Charcuterie* says he'd use a garlicky Toulouse sausage or a simple Italian sausage in a pinch but warns that the Spanish will come for us with pitchforks if we use something with fennel.

Fabada is a traditional dish from the region of Asturias, in northern Spain. It's also a region known for its cider, or *sidra*. We adapted a recipe that was shared with us by the good folks at Virtue Cider, who pair fabada with a glass of cold cider!

1 pound uncooked Asturian fabes de la Granja or Rancho Gordo Cassoulet (Tarbais) beans, picked over and rinsed

Pinch of saffron

1 pound cured ham hock

8 ounces tocino or pancetta

1 tablespoon extra-virgin olive oil

1 tablespoon Spanish pimentón (smoked paprika)

1 onion, halved

1 head garlic, halved crosswise

2 links (about ¾ pound total) morcilla (Spanish blood sausage)

8 ounces Spanish chorizo

Salt and freshly ground pepper

MAKES 4 TO 6 SERVINGS

Put the beans in a large pot and add cold water to cover by about 3 inches. Bring to a boil.

Meanwhile, in a small pan, toast the saffron over low heat for about 30 seconds while moving the pan constantly. Remove, cool, and crush with a spoon.

Once the beans are at a steady boil, add the ham hock, tocino, olive oil, crushed saffron, pimentón, onion, and garlic. Decrease the heat and cook, partially covered, until the beans are almost tender, 60 to 90 minutes. If the mixture starts to dry out, add 1 cup of water at a time. Avoid stirring the mixture too much or you will break up the beans; you can shake the pot instead.

Add the morcilla and chorizo (whole) and simmer, partially covered, for about 45 minutes. Continue adding water, 1 cup at a time, as needed. The stew should be brothy, and the beans and meat should remain separate from the broth, not disintegrated.

Once the beans are tender and the liquid is flavorful, remove and discard the onion and garlic, and remove the pot from the heat.

Carefully remove the meat and let it cool slightly. Slice the tocino, morcilla, and chorizo, and cut the ham off the bone and into large pieces. Return the meat to the mixture and cover for at least 10 minutes before serving. Season with salt and pepper.

BEANS & GRAINS

One of the culinary world's greatest duos is beans and rice. Or rice and beans, depending on whom you ask. In some countries, particularly in Latin America, the combination of rice and beans is considered a national dish, which is funny since rice is not from the Americas. The adoption of rice, and the blending of an indigenous ingredient with a foreign one, actually represents a lot of the Americas, for better and for worse. Happily, this is a delicious and nutritious marriage that's here to stay.

In addition to the beans and the rice meeting on your plate, some of the bean broth can be used to moisten and flavor the rice. Even when cooked, the rice will keep absorbing this flavorful bean broth.

The greatest hits of rice and beans would include Brazilian Feijoada, New Orleans Red Beans and Rice, Central American Gallo Pinto, and Cuban Moros y Cristianos or Congri. All of the dishes are traditional, and people tend to feel strongly about their regional dish. Tread lightly when suggesting to a Costa Rican that Gallo Pinto is made with red beans, unless you're on the eastern Caribbean coast.

You'll often hear about how rice with beans makes a "complete protein," leaving meat unnecessary to have a healthy diet. Rice and beans have complementing amino acids that make them wildly healthy, especially when you add vegetables to a varied diet. Some nutritionists wince at the term "complete protein" as it suggests that rice and beans might be all you need to be healthy. A diet full of beans, complex carbohydrates, fresh vegetables, and lots of variety can be considered healthy by any standard.

Rice isn't the only grain worth pairing with beans. Experiment with pasta, polenta, wild rice, farro, quinoa, and millet.

ALEXIS HANDELMAN'S WILD RICE AND HEIRLOOM BEAN SALAD FOR A CROWD

Vegetarians have traditionally been neglected on the holidays. Menus would often include meat or poultry, and vegetarians were lucky to find a mixed green salad, bad rolls, and dessert. In an effort to be more inclusive of all types of eaters, we asked a local chef, Alexis Handelman, to come up with something that would be substantial, delicious, and in the holiday spirit. She did, and this popular recipe and its infinite variations have made the season bright for many, not just those not eating meat.

The secret to a composed salad like this is to dress the components separately and then gently arrange them on a platter. It's a more dramatic presentation, and it ensures that each bite will have the proper amount of dressing.

FOR THE SALAD

2 cups cubed sugar pie pumpkin squash

½ red onion

Extra-virgin olive oil

Salt and freshly ground pepper

5 large Brussels sprouts

4 cups cooked, drained heirloom beans, such as Rancho Gordo Rebosero, Buckeye, Eye of the Goat, or Whipple

4 cups cooked wild rice, cooled

1 cup dried cranberries, rehydrated in water or brandy

1 fresh Fuyu persimmon, quartered and thinly sliced

⅓ cup baby arugula (rocket)

⅓ cup fresh flat-leaf parsley leaves

Preheat the oven to 400°F.

In a medium bowl, toss the squash cubes and onion half with a liberal amount of olive oil and season with salt and pepper. Transfer to a baking sheet and roast until tender, turning once, 15 to 20 minutes. Remove from the oven. Once the onion is cool enough to handle, cut it into ½-inch dice.

Meanwhile, separate the leaves from the Brussels sprouts, discarding the tough cores. In a steamer, steam the leaves until bright green and just tender, about 3 minutes.

To make the vinaigrette, in a bowl, whisk the olive oil, vinegars, mustard, and herbs until combined. Add salt and pepper to taste.

In a large bowl, combine the beans, wild rice, and diced onion. Mix in about half of the vinaigrette. Taste and adjust the seasoning with salt and pepper or more vinaigrette. Transfer to a large platter.

CONTINUED

FOR THE VINAIGRETTE

¾ cup extra-virgin olive oil

2 tablespoons red wine vinegar

2 tablespoons balsamic vinegar

1 to 2 teaspoons grainy mustard

2 tablespoons minced fresh herbs, such as lemon thyme, chervil, or marjoram

Salt and freshly ground pepper

GARNISH

¼ cup plus 2 tablespoons pomegranate seeds

1 cup toasted walnuts or pecans, chopped

MAKES 6 TO 8 SERVINGS

In another bowl, combine the roasted squash, Brussels sprouts, drained cranberries, persimmon, arugula, and parsley. Add about ¼ cup of the remaining vinaigrette and mix gently to combine. Taste and adjust the seasoning with salt and pepper or more vinaigrette. Scatter this mixture on top of the bean-rice mixture.

Sprinkle the pomegranate seeds and walnuts over the top of the salad and drizzle with the remaining vinaigrette.

COSTA RICAN GALLO PINTO

At its most simple, Gallo Pinto is rice and beans. They are cooked separately, but later they spend a good amount of time together so that the rice can absorb much of the bean broth, and it's really something special. This is another reason to make your beans from scratch with lots of broth, and you can try making a very rich rice by replacing the water with bean broth, or even a mix of bean broth and water.

As you experiment, you'll need to decide your favorite rice-to-bean ratio. It's tempting to just use half beans and half rice, but you may find that the beans take over, and you'll want a little more rice than beans, especially in a dish like Gallo Pinto or Congri, where the rice has been flavored with the bean broth. Ratios of 60/40 or 70/30 rice to beans tend to be more popular. But in the end, the correct ratio is the one that makes you happiest.

This is a very nutritious dish—especially when made with brown rice—that every student or young person living away from home should master. It's easy, delicious, easy on the budget, and even fun to make. Salsa Lizano is a kind of creamy Worcestershire sauce that is hard to find outside of Costa Rica. You can find it in import stores and Latin markets. It's very unique and easy to like, and in Costa Rica, required for this dish. You could use your favorite hot sauce or even a splash of Worcestershire sauce, but a Costa Rican would frown upon it.

3 tablespoons extra-virgin olive oil

1 yellow onion, diced

1 garlic clove, minced

1 small red bell pepper, seeded and chopped

1 cup uncooked white rice, rinsed and drained

2 cups water

Salt

3 cups cooked, drained black beans, such as Rancho Gordo Midnight Black beans, plus about ¾ cup bean broth reserved

In a large saucepan over medium heat, warm 1 tablespoon of the olive oil. Add half of the onion, the garlic, and half of the bell pepper and sauté until soft, about 5 minutes. Add the rice and sauté until opaque, about 2 minutes. Add the water and ½ teaspoon salt (or to taste). Increase the heat to high and bring to a boil. Decrease the heat to low, cover, and cook until the water is absorbed, about 20 minutes (depending on the type of rice you use).

In a large skillet over medium heat, warm the remaining 2 tablespoons olive oil. Add the remaining onion and sauté until soft, about 3 minutes. Add the cooked rice, stir to combine, and cook for 2 minutes.

CONTINUED

Salsa Lizano, chopped fresh
cilantro, sour cream, and/
or scrambled or fried eggs for
serving

MAKES 2 TO 4 SERVINGS

Add the cooked beans and their broth and the remaining bell
pepper. Stir well. Cook for about 5 minutes, until the rice is
"painted" by the bean broth. Taste and add more salt, if desired.
Serve with Salsa Lizano, cilantro, sour cream, scrambled or fried
eggs, or any combination you like.

VARIATION: NICARAGUAN GALLO PINTO

Substitute the black beans with red beans, such as Rancho Gordo
Domingo Rojo beans.

NEW ORLEANS RED BEANS AND RICE

There is something infectious about this dish. Many travelers have fond memories of trips to New Orleans, and Red Beans and Rice conjures up all the aromas, feelings, and tastes from that city.

New Orleans is the sort of place that makes you feel obligated to have fun and enjoy yourself. If you hook up with fun-loving friends, old or new, it's almost impossible to remain unmoved. Red Beans and Rice brings this joie de vivre back to our daily lives, even when we are away from New Orleans.

The background story of this dish is that on Mondays, which were wash days in New Orleans, housekeepers needed something that could be cooked low and slow for supper while they attended to the other domestic chores, most famously washing clothes. Meat would have been left over from the weekend, and so a great dish to accompany the meat was then created. There is beauty in a meal that can take care of itself while you do other things.

There are countless variations of this dish (and we're sure to offend some with ours), but our research and many, many pots of Red Beans and Rice led us to this recipe.

2 tablespoons olive oil

1 to 1½ pounds andouille sausage, cut into thick slices

2 yellow onions, chopped

5 garlic cloves, chopped

1 celery stalk, sliced

2 green bell peppers, seeded and deveined, then chopped

1 pound uncooked red beans, such as red kidney beans or Rancho Gordo Domingo Rojo beans, picked over and rinsed

2 bay leaves

2 teaspoons dried thyme

1 teaspoon pure chile powder

In a large Dutch oven, warm the olive oil over medium heat. Add the sausage slices and cook, stirring occasionally, until browned, about 6 minutes. With a slotted spoon, remove the sausage and set aside. Add the onions, garlic, celery, and bell peppers to the pot and cook until soft, stirring occasionally, about 10 minutes.

Add the beans, bay leaves, thyme, chile powder, cayenne, and enough water to cover the beans by about 2 inches. Bring to a strong boil and boil for 15 minutes. Decrease the heat to low or medium-low and simmer gently until the beans have started to soften but aren't fully cooked, usually just over 1 hour. Add salt and pepper to taste.

Add the reserved sausage to the pot along with the mustard. Continue to cook until the beans are soft and creamy, adding more water as needed to keep the beans covered, about an hour longer.

CONTINUED

NEW ORLEANS RED BEANS AND RICE, CONTINUED

½ teaspoon ground cayenne pepper, or to taste

Salt and freshly ground pepper

1 tablespoon Creole mustard (or other coarse-grain mustard)

Chopped fresh flat-leaf parsley and sliced green onions for garnish (optional)

Cooked white rice for serving

Vinegary hot sauce like Louisiana, Crystal, or Tabasco for serving

MAKES 6 TO 8 SERVINGS

When the beans are cooked, mash some of them against the side of the pot with a wooden spoon to thicken the liquid, or continue cooking until the liquid is more like a thick gravy than a thin soup.

Taste and adjust the seasoning as needed. Serve in soup bowls and garnish with chopped parsley and sliced green onions (if desired). Serve with warm rice and hot sauce.

CASAMIENTO SALVADOREÑO

The Salvadorian version of Gallo Pinto, or beans and rice, is called Casamiento and is mostly made with red beans. Red beans tend to be firmer and less creamy than black beans, but they also offer a good bean broth. This recipe is from Rancho Gordo employee Celene Cisneros; it's about half and half beans and rice, but many cooks think of Casamiento as a rice dish with beans rather than an equal partnership.

2 tablespoons vegetable oil

¼ cup chopped white onion

¼ cup chopped red or green bell pepper, seeded (optional)

2 cups cooked, drained red beans, such as Rancho Gordo Domingo Rojo beans, or black beans, such as Rancho Gordo Midnight Black beans, plus 1 cup bean broth reserved

2 cups cooked white rice

Salt to taste

MAKES 2 TO 4 SERVINGS

In a large skillet, heat the vegetable oil over medium heat. Add the onion and pepper (if using) and cook, stirring frequently, until the vegetables begin to soften but don't brown.

Add the beans and cook, stirring, for a few minutes. Add the bean broth and, when it boils, add the rice and stir well. Continue cooking until the mixture reaches your desired consistency. Add salt to taste.

MOROS Y CRISTIANOS

In Cuba, both the names Moros y Cristianos and Congri are used for virtually the same dish. Mostly the rice and beans are cooked together at the end, and the bean broth makes the dish particularly rich and delicious. In some places, the rice and beans are separate and only meet on your plate for a cleaner flavor. There's no right or wrong, but hopefully you'll try it both ways and see if one is more appealing to you.

Cubans are rather opinionated about their black beans. They use turtle beans, which have thin skins and produce a rich broth. There are some fun heirlooms that are black, like ayocote negro, but these wouldn't be a part of authentic Moros y Cristianos in Cuba.

4 lean bacon slices, chopped

Extra-virgin olive oil, as needed

1 white onion, diced

2 garlic cloves, smashed

1 green bell pepper, seeded, then diced

1 teaspoon pure New Mexican red chile powder

1 teaspoon dried Mexican oregano, preferably Rancho Gordo Oregano Indio

3 cups cooked, drained black beans, such as Rancho Gordo Midnight Black beans, plus about 1 cup bean broth reserved

Salt

About 2 cups cooked white rice

Lime wedges and hot sauce for serving

MAKES 2 TO 4 SERVINGS

In a large saucepan over medium-low heat, gently cook the bacon until the fat is rendered and the bacon is cooked through, about 10 minutes. You should have about 2 tablespoons of fat. If there is less, add olive oil as needed. Add the onion, garlic, and bell pepper and cook, stirring occasionally, until the bell pepper is soft, about 8 minutes. Add the red chile powder and oregano and stir until incorporated. Add the beans and their broth, stirring gently until combined. Decrease the heat to low and cook, stirring occasionally, for about 10 minutes to allow the flavors to mingle. Taste and add salt, if desired.

Spoon some of the rice and the beans alongside each other on individual plates. Serve immediately with lime wedges and hot sauce.

If you prefer your rice and beans combined: Prepare the recipe as directed above. Add the cooked white rice to the pot with the beans and simmer until you reach the desired consistency, adding more liquid if needed.

ARNAB CHAKLADAR'S CHANA MASALA

Traditionally, this dish is made from desi chana, a dark garbanzo-like legume that is sometimes called a black garbanzo even though they aren't really black. It shouldn't be confused with an Italian black garbanzo, which really is black. You could use desi chana or Italian black garbanzos—or even traditional garbanzos—for this dish from Indian chef Arnab Chakladar, who holds court at myannoyingopinions.com.

1 teaspoon coriander seed

3 teaspoons cumin (zeera) seed

¾ teaspoon fenugreek (methi) seed

1 teaspoon black peppercorns

1 pound uncooked garbanzo beans or desi chana, soaked overnight and drained, or 6 cups cooked, bean broth reserved

1 teaspoon baking soda (if using uncooked beans)

6 cups water (if using uncooked beans)

3 to 4 tablespoons neutral oil

The following whole spices for garam masala: 2 or 3 tej patta (dried Indian cassia leaves) or bay leaves; 5 cloves; 5 pods green cardamom

2 cups chopped red onion, plus 2 tablespoons for garnish

1 teaspoon black mustard seed

½ teaspoon ground ginger

¾ teaspoon ground turmeric

1 teaspoon chile powder (see Notes, page 190)

In a cast-iron skillet over low heat, toast the coriander seed, cumin seed, fenugreek seed, and peppercorns until fragrant. Set aside to cool.

If you're using uncooked beans: in a pressure cooker, cook the drained garbanzo beans with the baking soda and water until they are softened but still holding their shape (30 minutes in my old-school whistling Prestige pressure cooker; see Notes on page 190).

Heat the oil in a deep saucepan over medium heat and add the whole garam masala. As soon as the tej patta darkens, add the onion and sauté until it begins to brown, about 10 minutes.

Meanwhile, in a spice grinder, combine the toasted and cooled spices and the black mustard seed, ground ginger, turmeric, and chile powder and grind finely.

To the onion mixture, add the minced ginger and garlic and sauté until the raw aroma is gone. Add the freshly ground spices, stir to combine, and sauté for 1 to 2 minutes, stirring constantly to make sure nothing scorches.

CONTINUED

1 teaspoon peeled, minced fresh ginger, plus 1 tablespoon peeled, julienned fresh ginger for garnish

1 teaspoon minced garlic

A Ping-Pong-size ball of soft block tamarind, soaked in 1 cup hot water for 20 minutes and then squeezed by hand to extract all the goodness from the pulp (reserve strained liquid and discard pulp)

1 tablespoon jaggery or dark brown sugar

Salt

1 or 2 Thai chiles, slit, for garnish

Cooked white basmati rice or chapatis for serving (optional)

MAKES 4 TO 6 SERVINGS

Add the strained tamarind solution and the jaggery and season to taste with salt. Stir and bring to a high simmer. Add the cooked garbanzos with all the pot liquor to the pan, stir, return to a high simmer, and cook, uncovered, until thicker but still easily pourable.

Garnish with the chopped onion, julienned ginger, and Thai chiles and serve with rice or chapatis (if desired).

Notes from Chef Arnab Chakladar: If not pressure cooking the garbanzos, add water along the way while cooking them, ½ cup at a time. When the garbanzos are soft enough to serve, they should just be peeping over the pot liquor.

You can use a hot chile powder if you like, but I typically use the very mild Deggi Mirch.

In a sense, what you are doing in this recipe is finishing the garbanzos with a cumin-forward tamarind chutney (plus onions and other ingredients).

You can certainly garnish with a bit of cilantro too. And if you're like the missus, you might not want very much or any julienned ginger on there. Me, I can't get enough of it.

If you live in a city with South Asian groceries, those are the best places to purchase spices used in Indian cooking. The spices will be fresh, and you'll find a greater variety of spices than you would in the international aisle of a large grocery store. The staff may also be able to assist you with questions. Alternatively, you can purchase spices online at Kalustyan's or even Amazon. Look for Indian versions of spices such as cumin and coriander and also dried chiles, as they can be quite different from versions found elsewhere. While tamarind can be found in concentrate/paste form, the trade-off for the convenience is often astringency. It is far preferable to purchase seedless blocks of tamarind and soak and extract the pulp. A small block of tamarind will last forever in your refrigerator.

ITALIAN PASTA E FAGIOLI

Pasta e Fagioli is one of the world's great dishes. It was likely born of leftovers, artfully combined by a clever home cook, but now it's a tradition with many variants and a great way to feed a crowd with a one-pot meal. It needs only a salad to be complete.

Both beans and pasta release some starch when cooked, so the idea of adding them together is genius. It's not necessary to add chicken stock when you have good beans, pasta, aromatics, and a little time. As you prepare the beans, make sure you have plenty of liquid on hand when they are done as this will be the basis for your sauce.

2 tablespoons extra-virgin olive oil, plus more for drizzling

4 ounces pancetta, cubed or roughly chopped (optional)

1 medium onion, finely chopped

1 celery stalk, finely chopped

1 carrot, minced or sliced

1 garlic clove, minced

1 tablespoon tomato paste

½ teaspoon red pepper flakes, or to taste

4 cups bean broth (if you have less than 4 cups, make up the difference with another broth)

1 sprig rosemary

Salt and freshly ground pepper

8 ounces good-quality pasta (small tubular or shell shapes work well)

3 cups cooked, drained Rancho Gordo Cranberry or Borlotti Lamon beans, or white beans, such as Royal Corona or Marcella, bean broth reserved (see above)

Chopped fresh flat-leaf parsley for garnish (optional)

Grated pecorino or Parmesan cheese for serving

Lemon wedges for serving

MAKES 4 SERVINGS

In a large pot or Dutch oven, warm the olive oil over medium heat. Cook the pancetta (if using), stirring often, until fragrant and chewy. Using a slotted spoon, transfer the pancetta to a paper towel and set aside. If needed, add more olive oil. Add the onion, celery, carrot, and garlic and cook, stirring frequently, until the celery and carrot are soft and the onion is turning golden, 15 to 20 minutes. Add the tomato paste and red pepper flakes and cook for a few minutes until the paste is heated through and the tomato flavor is intensified.

Add the bean broth, rosemary sprig, and salt and pepper to taste. Simmer gently until the liquid starts to reduce, about 15 minutes.

Meanwhile, cook the pasta in a large stockpot in salted water according to package directions. Drain.

Add the drained pasta, beans, and reserved pancetta (if using) to the vegetable mixture, stir well, and gently cook for a few minutes to marry the flavors. Remove and discard the rosemary sprig.

Serve immediately with a splash of olive oil and a sprinkle of parsley (if desired). Pass around a bowl of grated pecorino or Parmesan cheese and lemon wedges for guests to help themselves.

POLENTA WITH BORLOTTI BEANS AND TOMATO SAUCE

There are many variations of Borlotti beans, but one of the most treasured is the variety from Lamon in the Veneto, about an hour north of Venice. They are the perfect match for a bed of soft polenta. If you're unable to find Borlotti Lamon beans, you can easily substitute any cranberry-type bean.

¼ cup olive oil

1 small onion, finely chopped

2 garlic cloves, minced

2 cups canned chopped tomatoes, preferably San Marzano, juice reserved

1 tablespoon red wine vinegar

2 tablespoons tomato paste

1 cup chicken or vegetable broth

4 fresh sage leaves, minced

Salt and freshly ground pepper

4 cups cooked, drained Rancho Gordo Borlotti Lamon or Cranberry beans

2 cups uncooked polenta

6 ounces pancetta, diced (optional)

Chopped fresh basil or parsley for garnish

Grated Parmesan cheese for serving

MAKES 6 SERVINGS

In a large pan, heat the olive oil over medium heat. Add the onion and garlic and cook, stirring, until the onion begins to soften, about 3 minutes. Stir in the tomatoes and red wine vinegar. In a small bowl, dissolve the tomato paste in the broth and add to the pan. Stir in the sage and season with salt and pepper. Simmer, stirring occasionally, until the sauce has thickened, 15 to 20 minutes.

Add the beans to the tomato sauce. Cook, stirring frequently, until heated through, about 15 minutes.

Meanwhile, cook the polenta (see page 266, or according to package instructions).

If using pancetta: Place the pancetta in a small saucepan over low heat. Cook, stirring frequently, until the pancetta is brown and crisp, about 15 minutes. Use a slotted spoon to transfer the pancetta to a paper towel to drain.

To serve, spoon the polenta into serving dishes. Ladle the beans over the polenta and top with the pancetta (if using). Garnish with fresh basil and serve with grated Parmesan.

LINGUINE WITH GARBANZO PUREE

Pureed chickpeas might seem like an odd sauce for pasta, but the effect is similar to pasta e fagioli. The starch and the creamy legumes are a great combination. This would be ideal for that last cup or so of garbanzos you might have lingering in the fridge.

¼ cup extra-virgin olive oil

1 large sprig rosemary

2 garlic cloves, peeled

1½ cups cooked, drained Rancho Gordo Garbanzo beans, plus some bean broth reserved

Salt and freshly ground pepper to taste

¼ cup heavy cream

8 ounces dried linguine

½ cup grated pecorino cheese

Large handful of fresh flat-leaf parsley, roughly chopped

Lemon wedges for serving

MAKES 4 SERVINGS

In a large pot, warm the olive oil over low heat. Add the rosemary and garlic and cook gently, stirring occasionally, for about 15 minutes. (The oil will become infused, and the smell will be incredible!) Remove the rosemary from the oil, and add the beans. Cook, stirring for 5 minutes. Remove about ½ cup beans and reserve.

Blend the mixture with an immersion blender until smooth (or let cool slightly and process in batches in a blender or food processor), adding enough bean broth to make a thin sauce. If you add too much liquid, increase the heat and reduce the sauce. Taste the sauce and add salt and pepper. Add the cream and stir to combine.

Cook the pasta according to package directions until it's just short of al dente, reserving about ½ cup of the pasta cooking water, then add the pasta to the sauce to finish cooking. Add the reserved garbanzos and a splash of pasta cooking water to loosen the sauce. Stir. Add the cheese and parsley, toss gently, and serve with lemon wedges.

PASTA E CECI
(GARBANZO AND PASTA SOUP)

The Italians love their ceci, or chickpeas, or garbanzos! This is a chickpea soup with pasta rather than a pasta e fagioli (pasta and beans) dish where both ingredients play equal roles. Make sure you save the garbanzo cooking liquid for an especially delicious soup base.

2 tablespoons olive oil, plus more for drizzling

1 large garlic clove, peeled and smashed

½ small yellow onion, chopped

2 celery stalks, chopped

2 tablespoons tomato paste

1 sprig rosemary, leaves only, chopped

½ teaspoon red pepper flakes, or to taste

2 cups cooked, drained Rancho Gordo Garbanzo beans, bean broth reserved (see below)

6 cups bean broth, vegetable broth, or water (or a combination)

6 ounces uncooked small tubular pasta, such as ditalini or tubetti

Salt and freshly ground pepper

Grated Parmesan cheese and chopped fresh parsley, for garnish

MAKES 6 SERVINGS

In a heavy-bottomed 6-quart soup pot or Dutch oven over medium-low heat, warm the olive oil. Add the garlic, onion, celery, and tomato paste and cook, stirring occasionally, until softened, about 10 minutes. Add the rosemary, red pepper flakes, garbanzos, and 6 cups of broth and bring to a boil over medium-high heat. Decrease the heat to medium-low and simmer, uncovered, about 30 minutes. Pass half the garbanzos through a food mill, or puree in a food processor or blender (or use an immersion blender in the pot). Return the puree to the soup.

Add the pasta to the soup and cook until the pasta is al dente, 10 to 12 minutes. Season to taste with salt and pepper. Ladle into individual soup bowls, and add a drizzle of olive oil and a sprinkle of Parmesan and parsley to each serving.

BAKED BEANS

Beans in the oven might seem counterintuitive, but low and slow seems to be the best technique for beans, whether it's a simple pot of beans with aromatics in a Dutch oven or dense New England baked beans with pork and maple syrup, preferably made in a clay crock. In France, cassoulet is the king of the slow-baked bean dishes, and in Greece, a dish of baked gigande beans smothered in tomatoes is simple comfort food at its best.

Most New England crocks are high fired as opposed to low fired. This means they're not quite so delicate outside of the oven, but they can't withstand a hot oven, so keep things low. If the bean pot were to break, the interior would look white as opposed to a low-fired pot, where the interior would look more like mud. Low-fired pots are more fragile, but they can handle a hotter oven, so make sure you know what kind of pot you're using.

Of course, an enameled cast-iron pot, like a Le Creuset, is also a smart choice. The enameled interior keeps things nonstick, even after hours of slow cooking.

SMITTEN KITCHEN'S PIZZA BEANS

In the Bean World, there are few recipes that get the attention of Deb Perelman's Smitten Kitchen Pizza Beans. It's a clever, simple idea, and yet you make it and you can't get over how good it is. You also kick yourself for not coming up with it on your own, but we can all be thankful that Deb made it a reality.

The attraction of pizza is the magic of tomatoes, cheese, and crust. This recipe has all that, but the beans replace the wheat crust. While Pizza Beans will not replace pizza, it's hard not to be a fan.

2 tablespoons olive oil

1 large onion, chopped

2 celery stalks, diced

1 large or 2 regular carrots, peeled and diced

Salt and freshly ground pepper or red pepper flakes

2 large garlic cloves, minced

¼ cup dry white or red wine (optional)

4 ounces curly kale leaves, chopped or torn

2¼ cups crushed tomatoes (one 28-ounce can minus 1 cup; reserve the rest for another use)

6 cups cooked, drained firm-tender giant white beans, such as Rancho Gordo Royal Corona beans (from 1 pound, or 2 cups, dried beans)

Up to ¾ cup vegetable broth

8 ounces mozzarella cheese, coarsely grated

⅓ cup grated Parmesan cheese

2 tablespoons roughly chopped fresh flat-leaf parsley, for garnish (optional)

MAKES 8 SERVINGS

Preheat the oven to 475°F.

In a braiser, shallow Dutch oven, or other ovenproof pan, heat the olive oil over medium-high heat. Add the onion, celery, and carrots. Season well with salt and pepper. Cook, stirring frequently, until the vegetables brown lightly, about 10 minutes. Add the garlic and cook for 1 minute.

Add the wine (if using) and use a wooden spoon to scrape up any stuck bits, then simmer until it disappears, 1 to 2 minutes. Add the kale and cook for 1 to 2 minutes, until collapsed, then add the tomatoes and bring to a simmer. Add the beans, and, if the mixture looks too dry or thick (canned tomatoes range quite a bit in juiciness), add up to ¾ cup broth, ¼ cup at a time. Decrease the heat to medium and simmer for about 10 minutes. Taste and adjust the seasonings as needed.

Sprinkle the beans first with the mozzarella, then the Parmesan, and bake for 10 to 15 minutes, until browned on top. If you're impatient and want a deeper color, you can run it under the broiler. Garnish with parsley (if desired).

CLAY-BAKED PACIFIC COD GRATIN WITH ONIONS AND WHITE BEANS

Clay is the perfect cooking vessel for a baked fish and bean recipe, but any gratin dish will do. Cod seems a little more forgiving than most fish, but it's a good idea to check for doneness regularly. Fish can be overcooked on a dime, and there are variations in the size of the fish, gratin dishes, and ovens that can affect the ultimate cooking time. But with a little bit of attention to timing, this dish can warm up any fall or winter gathering.

1 large white onion, thinly sliced

2 cups cooked, drained white beans, such as Rancho Gordo Marcella or Alubia Blanca beans

6 sprigs thyme

Extra-virgin olive oil

Salt and freshly ground pepper

1½ pounds boneless, skinless Pacific cod (3 to 4 fillets)

Chopped fresh herbs, such as parsley or dill (optional)

Lemon wedges for serving

MAKES 4 SERVINGS

Preheat the oven to 400°F.

In a baking dish, preferably a clay dish such as a Moroccan tagra or a gratin dish, arrange half of the onion slices in an even layer. Add the beans on top and spread them out in a layer. Top with the rest of the onion slices and the thyme sprigs. Drizzle with olive oil and sprinkle with salt and pepper. Place in the oven and bake until the onion has wilted some, about 10 minutes. Remove from the oven and carefully place the cod fillets on top. Drizzle generously with olive oil, and season with salt and pepper.

Bake, uncovered, for about 10 minutes, then carefully flip the fillets. Continue to bake until the cod flakes easily with a fork, 12 to 15 more minutes. Sprinkle with chopped herbs (if using) and serve directly from the dish, passing lemon wedges at the table.

CLASSIC FRENCH CASSOULET

At its most simple, cassoulet is a beans and pork casserole. It's a dish that's involved to make, but the rewards are tremendous. It has become a Christmas Day tradition in some families, but it's appropriate anytime you need a sweater to be comfortable.

There are traditionalists and there are free thinkers when it comes to cassoulet. Within regions that make cassoulet in France, there is little agreement about the precise way to make it—even within families there is discord. The bean used is not a stranger to controversy. Many believe that the best beans are Tarbais (from Tarbes), while others insist on coco beans. For years, many Americans believed that flageolet were the correct bean. We suggest treating the dish with respect and then just doing your best and following your instincts.

The bean broth is an important component of a cassoulet. French cooks will add up to four different types of pork, plus other flavorings, to the beans as they cook. This version simplifies the first step of cooking the beans.

We have been inspired by both Kate Hill (relaisdecamont.com) and Georgeanne Brennan (lavierustic.com) for their dedication to French cookery, and cassoulet in particular.

8 sprigs thyme

Handful of fresh parsley sprigs

10 black peppercorns

2 bay leaves

2 tablespoons olive oil

8 ounces fresh skin-on pork belly or pancetta, cut into large chunks

1 large yellow onion, chopped

2 pounds uncooked French Tarbais beans, Rancho Gordo Cassoulet Beans, or coco beans, picked over and rinsed

2 carrots, peeled and halved

2 celery stalks, halved

4 or 5 garlic cloves, peeled

Salt

Make a bouquet garni by placing the thyme sprigs, parsley sprigs, peppercorns, and bay leaves in the middle of a square of cheesecloth, bringing the ends together, and tying securely with kitchen string.

In a large, lidded Dutch oven (or other heavy casserole) over medium heat, warm the olive oil. Add the pork belly and cook until browned, about 10 minutes. Add the onion and sauté until softened, 5 to 7 minutes. Add the beans, bouquet garni, carrots, celery, and garlic.

Add enough water to cover the beans by about 2 inches. Bring to a boil over medium-high heat.

Decrease the heat to low and simmer, partially covered, until the beans are barely tender and the broth is flavorful, about 1 hour. Add salt to taste (1 or 2 teaspoons should be plenty).

5 or 6 whole confit duck legs, fat reserved, drumsticks and thighs separated

Red or white wine for deglazing pan, if needed

4 Toulouse sausages (or mild Italian sausage links), pricked with a toothpick in several places

MAKES 8 SERVINGS

In a skillet over medium-high heat, melt 1 tablespoon of reserved duck fat. Add the confit pieces, skin side down. (If your pan is small, you may need to do this in 2 batches.) Cook, turning often, until the skin is crisp and golden, about 10 minutes. If the duck skin sticks to the skillet, deglaze the pan with a splash of wine. Remove the duck legs and set aside.

Remove all but 1 tablespoon of the fat from the pan, reserving for another use. Add the sausages and cook, turning as needed, until they are cooked through and lightly browned, 12 to 15 minutes. Remove the sausages from the pan and cut each in half, reserving the fat for another use.

Preheat the oven to 300°F.

Remove the pork, vegetables, and bouquet garni from the beans. Discard the bouquet garni. Chop the vegetables and return them to the beans. Chop the pork belly and reserve it.

Use a slotted spoon to transfer enough beans to a French casserole or a wide, deep casserole or baking dish to make a 1-inch layer. Top with the confit and another layer of beans. Add the sausage, then cover with a final layer of beans. Sprinkle the top with the chopped pork belly, then ladle on enough of the bean broth to cover the beans by about ½ inch. Reserve the remaining broth for basting.

Place the casserole in the oven, uncovered. During the first hour of cooking, baste the top of the cassoulet with the reserved broth. After 1 hour of cooking, break through the crust with a wooden spoon. Repeat two or three more times, basting as needed with either the cooking liquid or the reserved broth.

Continue to bake until the beans are meltingly tender, the broth is bubbling along the sides, and a crispy browned crust has formed, about 2½ to 3 hours total.

To serve, bring the cassoulet directly to the table and scoop onto dinner plates. Each serving should include a piece of duck and sausage.

SARAH SCOTT'S NAPA VALLEY CASSOULET

Chef Sarah Scott often has a cassoulet dinner around Christmas. Sarah's version of cassoulet has firm roots in France, but it's a bit simpler yet no less satisfying than a traditional French version. Give yourself plenty of time to prepare the dish, and don't forget to let it rest a good 15 to 25 minutes before serving or it will be too hot to enjoy all the flavors.

FOR THE BEANS

1 pound uncooked French Tarbais or Rancho Gordo Cassoulet or Flageolet beans, picked over and rinsed

1 bay leaf

1 shallot

2 garlic cloves

3 sprigs thyme

2 sprigs fresh flat-leaf parsley

2 to 3 tablespoons salt

FOR THE PORK

1½ pounds boneless pork butt or shoulder, trimmed of excess fat and cut into 3-inch pieces

1 teaspoon salt

¼ teaspoon freshly ground pepper

4 tablespoons rendered duck fat

1 yellow onion, cut into ½-inch dice

5 garlic cloves, chopped

1 celery stalk, chopped

1 carrot, peeled and chopped

One 14-ounce can diced tomatoes, juice reserved

3 sprigs thyme

1 bay leaf

¼ cup dry white wine

To make the beans: Place the beans in a large pot and add water to cover twice the height of the beans. Make a bouquet garni by placing the bay leaf, shallot, garlic, thyme, and parsley in the middle of a square of cheesecloth, bringing the ends together, and tying securely with kitchen string. Add the bouquet garni to the pot and place the pot over medium-high heat. Bring to a boil, then decrease the heat to a simmer and cook, uncovered, until the beans are tender, 2 to 2½ hours.

Turn off the heat, add 2 tablespoons of the salt to the water, and stir gently. Taste and add more salt if needed. Remove the pot from the stove and let the beans cool to room temperature in the cooking broth. Discard the bouquet garni, then drain the beans, discard the cooking broth, and refrigerate the beans if not using right away. (The beans can be cooked up to 2 days ahead and kept in an airtight container in the refrigerator until ready to assemble the cassoulet.)

To make the pork: Season the pork with the salt and pepper. (Ideally, do this a day ahead of cooking the pork, cover the pork loosely, and refrigerate overnight.)

Preheat the oven to 350°F.

In a large pan, melt 2 tablespoons of the duck fat over medium-high heat. Add the onion, garlic, celery, and carrot and sauté until the vegetables are tender, 5 to 6 minutes. Transfer the vegetables to a medium roasting pan, spreading them evenly over the bottom. Evenly distribute the tomatoes and their juice over the vegetables.

FOR THE BROTH

4 cups chicken broth, preferably homemade

1 smoked ham hock

2 sprigs thyme

1 bay leaf

2 large shallots

TO FINISH

2 confit duck legs, skin removed

2 Toulouse sausages
(about 10 ounces total)

1 cup rendered duck fat

1½ cups coarse dried bread
crumbs, such as panko
(Japanese bread crumbs)

MAKES 4 TO 6 SERVINGS

CONTINUED

Scatter the thyme sprigs and bay leaf over the layered mixture, then place the seasoned pork chunks in an even layer on top. In the pan, melt the remaining 2 tablespoons duck fat over medium heat. Pour the wine and the melted duck fat evenly over the layered contents of the roasting pan.

Cover the contents of the pan with a sheet of parchment paper and then cover the pan with a sheet of aluminum foil, crimping it over the sides to seal. Bake until the pork is tender, 2½ to 3 hours.

Remove the pan from the oven and discard the foil and parchment. Using a slotted spoon, transfer the pork chunks to a plate and set aside. Drain the vegetable mixture through a fine-mesh sieve, capturing the liquid in a bowl or other vessel. Reserve the liquid. Discard the thyme and bay leaf, transfer the vegetables to a food processor, and puree until smooth. Stir the puree into the beans. Skim off and discard any fat from the surface of the liquid.

To make the broth: Combine the chicken broth, ham hock, thyme, bay leaf, and shallots in a medium saucepan over high heat. Bring to a boil, then decrease the heat to low and simmer for 1 hour.

Strain the broth through a fine-mesh sieve into a bowl. Reserve the broth and the ham hock and discard the rest of the ingredients. Add the reserved liquid from cooking the pork to the broth.

When the ham hock is cool, remove the meat and discard the fat, bone, and skin. Cut or shred the meat into small bite-size pieces. Add the meat to the reserved pork chunks and stir together gently.

SARAH SCOTT'S NAPA VALLEY CASSOULET, CONTINUED

Preheat the oven to 325°F.

To finish, pull off the meat from the confit duck legs in large chunks, discard the bones, and set the meat aside.

Bring a large saucepan of water to a boil. Prick the sausages with a fork three or four times. Carefully slip them into the boiling water, decrease the heat to a gentle simmer, and poach the sausages until firm and cooked through, 8 to 10 minutes. Remove the sausages from the water, let cool, and cut each into 4 pieces.

In a large pan, melt 2 tablespoons of the duck fat over medium heat. Add the sausage pieces and brown on all sides. Transfer to a plate and set the pan aside.

Put one-third of the beans in the bottom of a 3-quart cassoulet dish or a 9 by 13-inch baking dish. Tuck the pieces of duck confit and pork into the beans. Add half of the remaining beans and tuck the sausages into this second layer of beans. Spread the remaining beans on top. Pour enough of the broth into the dish to fill to just below the rim.

Place the bread crumbs in a bowl. In the reserved pan, melt ½ cup of the remaining duck fat over medium-low heat. Pour the duck fat over the crumbs and toss to combine. Spread the crumbs evenly over the top layer of beans.

Bake for 1½ hours, then remove the dish from the oven. Using a large spoon, break through the surface of the cassoulet, turning up a small area of the top crust that has formed. If the broth has evaporated and the cassoulet seems dry, add more broth. Melt the remaining duck fat, drizzle it evenly over the surface, and return to the oven.

Continue to bake until the juices are bubbling around the edges and a deep golden crust has formed on the surface, 1½ to 2 hours. Remove from the oven and let cool for 15 to 25 minutes before serving.

GIGANDES PLAKI
(GREEK BAKED BEANS)

Greek gigande beans are a kissing cousin to corona beans. They are a little starchier (but not much), and the two beans can be substituted without concern.

It's always interesting to note that here in the United States, some complain about it being too hot to cook beans, but some of the best, most innovative bean dishes come from warm climates. Gigandes Plaki is no exception.

You can substitute lima beans if needed. They are very different but no less delicious.

½ cup extra-virgin olive oil, plus more for drizzling

1 sweet white onion, finely chopped

2 garlic cloves, minced

¼ cup canned tomato puree

2 large, ripe tomatoes (about 1 pound), chopped

1 teaspoon dried Greek oregano

Pinch of ground cinnamon

2 tablespoons chopped fresh flat-leaf parsley or dill, plus more for serving

Salt and freshly ground pepper

3 to 4 cups cooked, drained gigande beans, or Rancho Gordo Royal Corona or Large White Lima beans

MAKES 4 TO 6 SIDE DISH SERVINGS

Preheat the oven to 350°F.

Heat the olive oil in a large skillet over medium heat. Add the onion and garlic and cook until softened but not browned, about 10 minutes. Add the tomato puree, cook for another minute or so, then add the chopped tomatoes, oregano, cinnamon, and parsley. Cook for 2 to 3 minutes. Season generously with salt and pepper, then stir in the beans.

Transfer the mixture to a large ovenproof dish. Drizzle olive oil over the top, then bake, uncovered, until the beans are soft and creamy and the sauce has thickened, 45 minutes to 1 hour. Let cool, then scatter with additional parsley and drizzle with more olive oil to serve.

TUSCAN-STYLE BAKED CANNELLINI BEANS WITH TOMATOES AND SAGE

You might assume that rosemary makes something more "Tuscan," but sage is really the herb of choice. Sage and tomatoes create a partnership that makes white beans happy—or at least delicious. Our Marcella beans, perfect in this dish, are delicate and benefit from the low, gentle heat of the oven, but if you prefer, you can cook them on the stovetop, drain them, and then add the tomato sauce.

5 tablespoons good-quality extra-virgin olive oil, preferably Italian, plus more for drizzling

2 garlic cloves, crushed, plus 2 garlic cloves, minced

8 ounces uncooked cannellini beans, such as Rancho Gordo Marcella beans, picked over and rinsed

1 sprig sage leaves, plus 3 chopped fresh sage leaves

Freshly ground pepper

½ cup canned crushed tomatoes, preferably from Italy

1 tablespoon tomato paste

½ teaspoon red pepper flakes (optional)

Salt

MAKES 4 SIDE DISH SERVINGS

Preheat the oven to 250°F.

In a medium to large pot with an ovenproof lid (preferably an earthenware pot), warm 2 tablespoons of the olive oil over medium heat. Add the crushed garlic and cook until fragrant, about 2 minutes. Add the beans, sage sprig, a few grinds of pepper, and enough water to cover the beans by 2 inches. Increase the heat to high and bring to a boil. Boil for 10 minutes.

Cover the pot and carefully place in the oven. Cook until the beans are tender but still have a bite (al dente), 1 to 2 hours. Check the beans often and add more boiling water as needed to keep them covered.

Meanwhile, warm the remaining 3 tablespoons olive oil in a large skillet or Dutch oven over medium heat. Add the minced garlic, chopped sage leaves, tomatoes, tomato paste, and pepper flakes (if using) and cook for about 5 minutes.

When the beans are soft, drain them and add to the tomato sauce, stirring gently to combine. Cook over low heat for about 10 minutes. Season to taste with salt and additional pepper.

Before serving, drizzle the beans with olive oil.

HEIRLOOM BEAN AND CARAMELIZED FENNEL GRATIN

A good party can benefit from a large casserole. Much of the work can be completed ahead, and the final cooking can be done as guests arrive and enjoy drinks and appetizers. This casserole and a big salad would make a perfect dinner.

If you'd like to enjoy this gratin as a rich side with meat, choose something simple and grilled.

2 large fennel bulbs, trimmed

6 tablespoons extra-virgin olive oil

1 leek, rinsed and chopped

4 garlic cloves, finely chopped

2 bay leaves

4 to 6 sprigs thyme, leaves stripped and stems discarded

½ cup white wine

1 cup vegetable broth

3 to 4 cups cooked, drained white or light beans, such as Rancho Gordo Yellow Eye beans

Zest of 1 lemon, plus a squeeze of lemon juice

Salt and freshly ground pepper

Minced fresh basil for garnish

FOR THE TOPPING

2 tablespoons (¼ stick) butter or olive oil

½ cup dried bread crumbs

½ cup finely grated Parmesan cheese

MAKES 4 SERVINGS

Preheat the oven to 400°F.

Cut the fennel bulbs in half; cut crosswise into slices about ½ inch thick, then roughly chop. Rinse well and set aside.

In a large skillet over medium heat, warm 2 tablespoons of the olive oil. Add the leek and sauté until soft and caramelized, about 10 minutes. Remove the leek from the pan and set aside. Add the remaining 4 tablespoons olive oil to the pan, then add the fennel, garlic, bay leaves, and thyme. Sauté until the fennel is soft and beginning to turn golden, about 10 minutes. Add the wine and broth. Stir, scraping the bottom of the pan to deglaze. Cook for about 5 minutes to reduce. Stir in the leek, beans, and lemon zest and juice. Taste and season generously with salt and pepper. Remove and discard the bay leaves. Transfer the mixture to a wide baking dish or gratin.

Prepare the topping: In a small skillet, melt the butter over medium-low heat. Add the bread crumbs and cheese. Stir to combine. Sprinkle the mixture over the casserole in the baking dish.

Cover the dish with aluminum foil and bake until beginning to bubble, 30 to 40 minutes. Uncover and bake until the top is golden, 15 to 20 minutes. Remove from the oven and let sit for 10 minutes before serving. Garnish with fresh basil.

NEW ENGLAND BAKED BEANS

It seems even non-bean people love baked beans. Even if your family didn't have this tradition, baked beans are nostalgic. They're rich and maybe a little indulgent, unless you've been out chopping trees all day or collecting maple syrup in the cold and you want to come home to something substantial, sweet, and rich.

There are lots of regional variations. Some places use yellow eye beans (not to be confused with black-eyed peas), others use Jacob's Cattle or cranberry beans, while some use navy, great northern, or European soldier beans. We prefer yellow eyes over white beans because they add more bean flavor.

The type of sweetener also varies by region. We've settled on maple syrup and brown sugar for our version, and offer some variations below.

The traditional process of cooking long and slow in a crock keeps the beans solid and whole because of all the acids used. Tomatoes and molasses will inhibit softness, but time will win in the end.

1 pound uncooked yellow eye beans, or navy or great northern beans, picked over and rinsed

8 ounces thick-cut bacon or salt pork, cut into chunks (if using salt pork, rinse well and pat dry to remove excess salt)

1 small onion, chopped

3 tablespoons brown sugar

3 tablespoons maple syrup

2 tablespoons ketchup

2 teaspoons ground mustard

Salt and freshly ground pepper to taste

MAKES 6 TO 8 SIDE DISH SERVINGS

In a large pot, combine the beans and enough water to cover them by about 2 inches. Place over medium-high heat, bring to a boil, and boil for 10 to 15 minutes. Decrease the heat to low and simmer gently until the beans are nearly cooked but still slightly al dente, about 1 hour. Drain the beans and reserve the broth.

Preheat the oven to 300°F.

In a Dutch oven over medium heat, cook the bacon until golden, about 5 minutes. Add the onion and cook until soft, about 5 minutes. In a bowl, stir together the brown sugar, maple syrup, ketchup, and mustard. Add about 1 cup of water and stir well.

Add the maple mixture to the bacon and onion and stir to combine. Add the cooked beans and stir gently. Add enough bean broth and/or water to just cover the beans. Taste and season with salt and pepper. Remember that the pork will contribute to the saltiness as the beans bake.

Increase the heat and bring the beans to a boil, then turn off the heat, cover, and bake for about 2 hours. Check occasionally, adding hot water as needed. Uncover, then bake for about another 2 hours, until the beans are dark and flavorful and a nice crust has formed over the top. You may need to add additional water if the beans get dry.

VARIATION: VERMONT BAKED BEANS

In Vermont, maple syrup is the favored sweetener. Omit the brown sugar and ketchup, and use ⅔ cup maple syrup.

VARIATION: BOSTON BAKED BEANS

Molasses separates Boston Baked Beans from others. Boston was a major producer of molasses in the 1900s (in 1919, a giant tank of molasses burst open in Boston's North End, spilling more than two million gallons in the streets of Boston!). Omit the maple syrup and brown sugar, and use ½ cup molasses.

MARGARET ROACH'S RATHER FAMOUS VEGETARIAN BAKED BEANS

Margaret Roach is a renowned gardening expert and bean lover. She shared this recipe on *The Martha Stewart Show* in 2011 (and was kind enough to give Rancho Gordo and heirloom beans a shout-out). It's a clever recipe and brings home the idea that the best thing about baked beans is the beans, not necessarily the pork.

Margaret has written several gardening books, and her website, *A Way to Garden*, often features very good food—and very good bean recipes, in particular.

1 pound uncooked cranberry, navy, or yellow eye beans, picked over and rinsed

¼ cup molasses, preferably organic

¼ cup grade A medium-amber maple syrup

¼ cup grainy mustard

6 fresh, peeled or canned whole plum tomatoes, chopped

2 tablespoons olive oil

2 medium yellow onions, quartered and sliced

Boiling water

Coarse salt and freshly ground pepper

MAKES 6 TO 8 SIDE DISH SERVINGS

Preheat the oven to 325°F.

Place the beans in a large pot, add enough water to cover, and let soak overnight. Drain and return the beans to the pot. Add enough water to cover, place over medium-high heat, and simmer for 30 minutes. Drain and transfer to a large bowl. Stir in the molasses, maple syrup, mustard, and tomatoes. Set aside.

Coat the bottom of a Dutch oven or a 9 by 13-inch high-sided baking dish with the olive oil. Add the onions and top with the bean mixture. Add enough boiling water to cover the bean mixture by 1 inch. Place the lid on the Dutch oven or cover your baking dish with parchment paper and aluminum foil. Transfer to the oven and bake until the beans are softened, about 1½ hours, checking the water level and adding more as necessary.

Uncover the beans and continue baking until thick and syrupy, about 45 minutes. Season with salt and pepper and serve.

HEIRLOOM BEAN AND CHEESE CASSEROLE WITH MUSHROOM CARNITAS

The following technique for mushroom "carnitas" comes from the blog *He Cooks, She Cooks*. It's counterintuitive and delicious at the same time. If you are a mushroom fan, this is a handy technique to know about. There's a real satisfaction in taking everyday button mushrooms and turning them into something so wonderful and useful.

2 cups sliced button mushrooms

2 garlic cloves, whole, plus 2 garlic cloves, minced

4 tablespoons extra-virgin olive oil

Sea salt

1 teaspoon dried Mexican oregano, preferably Rancho Gordo Oregano Indio

½ cup bread crumbs

1 teaspoon dried thyme

6 ounces canned whole peeled tomatoes, plus ½ cup juice reserved

2 cups cooked, drained Rancho Gordo Eye of the Goat beans or other brown beans

8 to 10 small fresh mozzarella balls (bocconcini)

MAKES 4 TO 6 SERVINGS

In a large saucepan, combine the mushrooms, whole garlic cloves, 2 tablespoons of the olive oil, 1 teaspoon sea salt, and the oregano. Add enough water to not quite cover the mushrooms. Bring to a hard boil over high heat. Decrease the heat to a gentle simmer and cook until the liquid has mostly evaporated, about 15 minutes, stirring to avoid scorching. Watch carefully: once evaporation starts, things happen quickly. The mushrooms will start to sauté in the residual oil. Keep stirring until the mushrooms are golden brown. Remove from the heat and set aside.

Preheat the oven to 375°F.

In a small bowl, combine the remaining 2 tablespoons olive oil, the bread crumbs, and thyme. Mix well.

Drain and roughly chop the tomatoes. In a small casserole, combine the tomatoes, reserved tomato juice, beans, minced garlic, and reserved mushrooms. Stir well. Taste and add more salt if needed, but the beans and mushrooms are likely to already be well salted. Arrange the mozzarella balls on the top of the casserole and push them down into the liquid. Sprinkle with the seasoned bread crumbs.

Bake, uncovered, for about 45 minutes, but start checking after 30 minutes. The liquid should be bubbling and the cheese starting to melt.

CHEESY BLACK BEAN AND CORN SKILLET BAKE

If you play your cards right, you might have these ingredients on hand already and can throw them in a skillet for a very easy meal. You can place the hot skillet right on the table, serve with warm tortillas, and let diners dig in. Even if you don't have everything on hand, it's still an easy and satisfying dish.

For an appetizer for a crowd, omit the eggs and serve this as a bean dip, with hearty tortilla chips on the side. Don't skimp on the cheese!

3 tablespoons extra-virgin olive oil

4 garlic cloves, sliced

½ yellow onion, chopped

1 jalapeño chile, seeded and minced

1 teaspoon dried Mexican oregano, preferably Rancho Gordo Oregano Indio

¼ teaspoon red pepper flakes (optional)

2 tablespoons tomato paste

Corn kernels, from 2 ears of corn (about 1 cup)

3 cups cooked, drained black beans, plus ½ cup bean broth reserved

Salt and freshly ground pepper

4 eggs (optional)

1 cup grated Fontina or manchego cheese

Chopped fresh flat-leaf parsley or cilantro for garnish

Warm tortillas or thick tortilla chips for serving

MAKES 4 SERVINGS

Preheat the oven to 325°F.

In a 10-inch ovenproof skillet over medium heat, heat the olive oil. Add the garlic and cook until lightly golden, about 1 minute. Stir in the onion, jalapeño, oregano, pepper flakes (if using), and tomato paste and cook for 30 seconds, reducing the heat as needed to prevent the garlic from burning. Add the corn and cook for a few minutes to combine the flavors.

Add the beans, bean broth, and generous pinches of salt and pepper, and stir to combine. If adding eggs: make 4 small hollows in the bean mixture as best you can; carefully crack an egg into each hollow. Sprinkle the cheese evenly over the top. Bake until the eggs are just starting to set but still jiggly, 8 to 10 minutes. Serve immediately, sprinkled with fresh parsley alongside warm tortillas or chips.

GREEK SLOW-BAKED GARBANZOS WITH TOMATOES AND PEPPERS

If you've been a follower of Dan Buettner's Blue Zones, you might be aware of the Greek island of Ikaria, also known as the place where people forget to die. Buettner has tracked places and lifestyles with extended longevity, and, as you might have guessed, one of the factors that help extend life is the consumption of beans.

Diane Kochilas wrote a wonderful book of Ikarian cuisine, *Ikaria: Lessons on Food, Life, and Longevity from the Greek Island Where People Forget to Die*. This is a slightly adapted version of a casserole from that book, and it has been a hit on its own with a green salad for a perfect summer lunch or as a side dish for proteins. The ingredients meld together to create a delicious sauce. Once tomatoes are in season, this dish goes into heavy rotation, but please don't use anemic tomatoes!

8 ounces uncooked garbanzo beans, picked over and rinsed

3 bay leaves

6 sprigs thyme

2 sprigs rosemary

Salt

3 large red onions, halved and sliced

3 garlic cloves, thinly sliced

1 each red, green, and orange bell peppers, stemmed, seeded, and sliced into ¼-inch rings

2 celery stalks, thinly sliced

2 or 3 large tomatoes, sliced

½ cup extra-virgin olive oil

Freshly ground pepper

MAKES 4 TO 6 SERVINGS

In a large saucepan over high heat, combine the garbanzo beans with 1 of the bay leaves and enough water to cover them by about 2 inches. Bring to a rapid boil and boil for 15 minutes. Decrease the heat to medium-low and gently simmer the beans until they're almost soft, about 1 to 1½ hours. Drain the beans and reserve the cooking liquid.

Preheat the oven to 325°F.

In a wide, ovenproof pan, like a cazuela, add the drained garbanzo beans followed by enough of the reserved cooking broth to reach one-third of the way up the beans. Add the thyme, rosemary, and the remaining 2 bay leaves and season lightly with salt.

Atop the garbanzo beans, layer the onions, garlic, bell peppers, celery, and tomatoes. Drizzle with the olive oil. Cover the pan with a lid, if you have one; otherwise, cover with a piece of parchment paper and then aluminum foil.

Bake for 2½ hours. Uncover and continue baking another 30 minutes. The liquid should be absorbed and the top just starting to deeply brown. Remove from the oven and cool to warm or room temperature. Remove and discard the bay leaves and herb sprigs. Grind plenty of black pepper over the top and serve.

MOROCCAN CHICKPEA TAGINE

A tagine is a dish and also a clay cooking vessel. As a vessel, it has a tall, cone-shaped or domed lid that very cleverly recirculates moisture. You can easily make one with a shallow skillet and lid, but an unglazed clay tagine is a marvel. Moroccan and Mediterranean food expert Paula Wolfert says that a pot or tagine without any glaze retains the memory of everything you've ever cooked in it. It's a soft, gentle memory, but it's there, so it's best to dedicate each clay tagine to a rough category of food. Maybe one for vegetables and chicken and another for fish.

This recipe is a very typical chicken tagine—only there's no chicken. We've switched the chicken for cooked garbanzos, and it's possibly even better!

Eat with flatbread or plain white rice.

3 tablespoons olive oil

1 red onion, cut into medium dice

3 garlic cloves

Salt

2-inch piece fresh ginger, peeled and grated

½ teaspoon saffron, in a little warm water

1 teaspoon ground cinnamon

Juice of ½ lemon

1 small preserved lemon, rind sliced into thin slivers and pulp coarsely chopped

2 tablespoons chopped fresh parsley

2 tablespoons chopped fresh cilantro, plus more for garnish

3 cups cooked, drained garbanzo beans, plus ¾ cup bean broth reserved

⅓ cup Kalamata olives, pitted and halved

Freshly ground pepper

MAKES 2 TO 4 SERVINGS

Heat a tagine or heavy-bottomed, shallow, lidded pan over low heat and add the olive oil, followed by the onion. Mash the garlic with ½ teaspoon salt and add to the pan. Cook until fragrant, about 5 minutes.

Add the ginger, saffron water, cinnamon, lemon juice, preserved lemon (rind and pulp), parsley, and cilantro and cook, stirring, for 2 minutes to let the flavors combine.

Arrange the garbanzos on top and scatter over the olives. Pour the broth into the pan, cover tightly, and simmer very gently for about 45 minutes, until the mixture is cooked down.

Season to taste with pepper and additional salt. Garnish with cilantro.

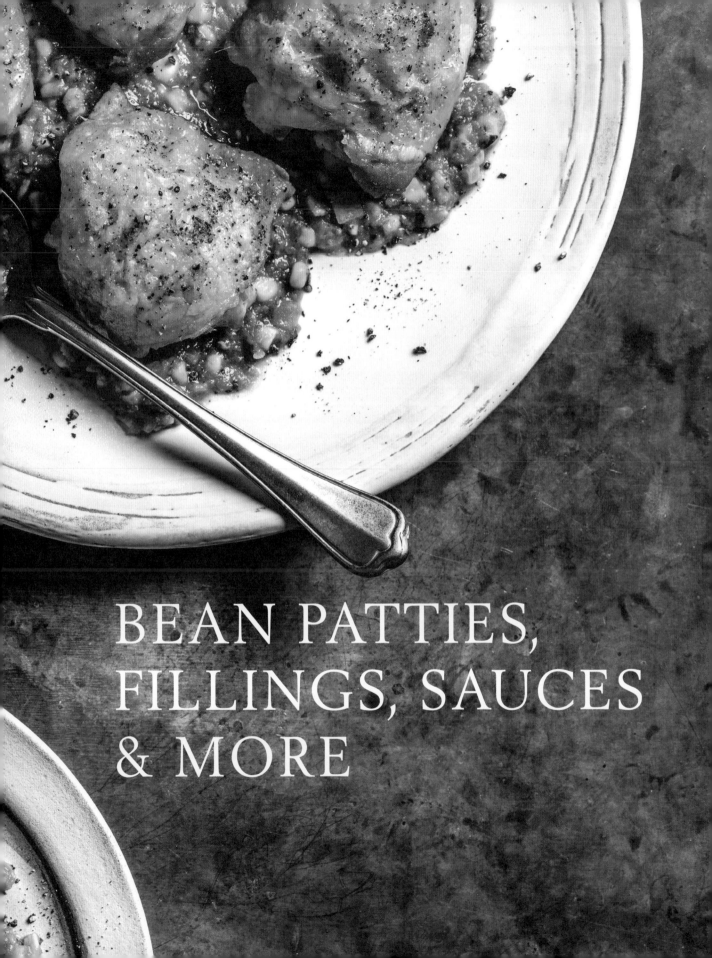

BEAN PATTIES,
FILLINGS, SAUCES
& MORE

Americans love burgers. They love their beef patties, but they also love bean patties.

Taking mashed-up beans and shaping them into patties is not quite as simple or intuitive as you might imagine, so we've experimented and toiled to create bean burgers that can stand up proudly to anything else on the grill. Another beloved dish in the crisp-fried bean patty category is, of course, falafel. Creamy tahini sauce is a perfect match for the golden balls of garbanzo bean goodness. We love the idea of bean patties because the toppings and accompaniments are flexible and according to your preference. Try to break free from tradition and let your imagination run wild.

Besides patties, you'll find plenty of other memorable bean dishes in this chapter, from tortillas smothered in pureed beans (enfrijoladas) to Mexican beans on toast (molletes) to chicken thighs resting in a poblano-bean sauce.

Then there is possibly my favorite bean dish of all: a simple bowl of heirloom beans topped with something flavorful and fantastic. If you've learned anything from this book, we hope it's that good heirloom beans don't need much to shine—a dollop of fried ricotta, some pickled vegetables, or a spoonful of fresh Italian salsa verde.

NORMAN ROSE TAVERN'S BLACK BEAN BURGER

A lot of Americans love eating burgers, and in their honor, we're offering the best version of the bean burger we've had. It's from Napa's celebrated Norman Rose Tavern, and it's been on the menu since they opened in 2009.

Most bean burger recipes seem to favor black beans, probably because of the texture. You might experiment with buckeyes (also known as Yellow Indian Woman) or King City Pinks, neither of which are black but have a similar texture. This recipe uses eggs to bind the ingredients, but an egg substitute would also work.

5 tablespoons vegetable or grapeseed oil

6 tablespoons finely chopped onion

2 garlic cloves, chopped

2 cups cooked, well-drained Rancho Gordo Midnight Black beans

1 cup cooked, drained barley (cooked without salt)

1 cup panko bread crumbs

2 tablespoons minced fresh cilantro

2 tablespoons minced fresh parsley

2 tablespoons minced fresh thyme

1 teaspoon ground cumin

1 teaspoon paprika

1 teaspoon ground coriander

1 teaspoon freshly ground pepper

2 teaspoons salt, or to taste

2 eggs, lightly beaten, or a vegan egg substitute if preferred

8 burger buns

For topping: sliced cheese, sliced tomatoes and onions, lettuce, pickles, ketchup, mustard, aioli (optional)

MAKES 8 PATTIES

In a small skillet over medium-low heat, warm 1 tablespoon of the oil. Add the onion and sauté until lightly caramelized, 4 to 6 minutes. Add the garlic and cook for another minute. Set aside.

Puree 1¼ cups of the beans in a food processor.

In a bowl, mix the remaining ¾ cup whole beans along with the bean puree, onion mixture, barley, bread crumbs, cilantro, parsley, thyme, cumin, paprika, coriander, and pepper. Taste and add salt if needed (it will depend on how salty your beans are). Stir in the eggs.

Form the mixture into 8 burger patties, about 1 inch thick, and refrigerate for at least 4 hours. This will allow the burgers to firm up a bit and the seasonings to develop.

Preheat the oven to 200°F.

In a large nonstick pan or cast-iron skillet over medium heat, heat 2 tablespoons of the oil until shimmering. Add 4 patties and cook, swirling the pan occasionally, until well browned and crisp on the first side, about 5 minutes. Carefully flip the patties and cook until the second side is browned, about 5 minutes longer, adding a slice of cheese on top (if desired). Place the cooked burgers on a rack set in a rimmed baking sheet and keep warm in the oven. Add the remaining 2 tablespoons oil to the pan and cook the remaining burgers.

Serve the burgers on buns with your choice of toppings.

FALAFEL WITH TAHINI SAUCE

Let's face it: fried things are great, and falafel are no exception. A crunchy, satisfying exterior and a softer, savory interior. A cooling tahini sauce for the final touch makes the falafel somewhat magical.

Falafel aren't pre-cooked. The cooking comes from deep-frying, so this is the one time when you really need to soak, no matter how fresh or old your garbanzos.

1 cup uncooked Rancho Gordo Garbanzo beans, soaked in water for 6 to 8 hours, drained

1 cup fresh parsley leaves, chopped

1 cup fresh cilantro leaves, chopped

1 cup fresh mint leaves, chopped

4 green onions, including green tops, roughly chopped

½ medium yellow onion, roughly chopped

2 garlic cloves, chopped

2 teaspoons ground cumin

¾ teaspoon baking soda

2 teaspoons salt, or to taste

Freshly ground pepper

Canola or sunflower oil for frying

FOR THE TAHINI SAUCE

½ cup tahini

3 tablespoons fresh lemon juice

2 garlic cloves, chopped

Up to ½ cup cold water

Salt and freshly ground pepper to taste

½ cup chopped fresh parsley leaves

Hummus, baba ghanoush, pita, cucumber, tomato, pickled vegetables, fresh herbs, and/or lettuce for serving (optional)

MAKES 12 FALAFEL

In a food processor, combine the garbanzos, parsley, cilantro, mint, green onions, yellow onion, garlic, cumin, baking soda, salt, and pepper to taste. Puree, scraping down the sides of the bowl as needed, until the mixture is consistent and holds together to form a ball. This mixture can be made ahead of time and refrigerated for up to 1 day.

Have ready a large baking sheet. Using two spoons or damp hands, shape the falafel mixture into twelve 2-inch balls. Arrange the balls on the baking sheet and refrigerate for about 20 minutes. Pour the canola oil into a large skillet or Dutch oven to a depth of 2 inches. Heat over medium-high heat until a deep-fry thermometer reads 300°F. In batches, carefully drop the falafel balls into the hot oil and fry until golden brown, about 5 minutes.

Using a slotted spoon, transfer the cooked falafel to paper towels to drain.

To make the tahini sauce: In a small food processor, puree the tahini, lemon juice, and garlic. Add a little bit of cold water at a time and blend again until you reach a consistency similar to salad dressing. Taste and season with salt and pepper. Stir in the parsley. (The sauce will thicken as it sits, so you may need to add more water to thin it out before serving.)

Serve the falafel with the tahini sauce and desired accompaniments.

ENFRIJOLADAS
(TORTILLAS IN A BLACK BEAN SAUCE)

Enchiladas are made with chiles. Enmoladas are made with mole. Enfrijoladas are made with a bean sauce. This is a great way to use up those last cups of beans and their broth tucked away in the refrigerator.

Enfrijoladas can be served with poached chicken and cheese or simply dipped and rolled, halved, or quartered and enjoyed as pure beans and corn. Oaxaca is probably the most famous for this dish, often served as breakfast, but you do see it all around Mexico. Black turtle beans are the most traditional, but there's nothing to stop you from experimenting with any dark or medium bean instead.

2 tablespoons good-quality lard or olive oil

1 white onion, sliced into thin rings, a few rings reserved for garnish

3 garlic cloves, minced

3 cups cooked, drained Rancho Gordo black beans, such as Midnight Black or Santanero Negro Delgado, or Rio Zape beans, broth reserved

2 cups bean, chicken, or vegetable broth, plus more if needed

⅓ cup canola oil

12 corn tortillas

½ cup crumbled queso fresco or farmer cheese

Chopped fresh cilantro for garnish (optional)

Sour cream, Mexican crema, or crème fraîche (optional)

MAKES 6 SERVINGS

In a large saucepan over low heat, melt the lard. Add the onion and cook gently until the onion slices are almost falling apart. Add the garlic and cook until it's soft. Add the beans and broth and cook until the beans are warmed through. Transfer the bean mixture to a food processor and process until smooth. Transfer the bean mixture back to the saucepan. (You can also use an immersion blender to puree the beans in the pot.) If you prefer texture, you can mash the beans with a machacadora (wooden bean masher) or a potato ricer until the mixture is somewhat smooth but still has a little texture. Keep warm over low heat, stirring occasionally. Add more broth if the beans seem too thick.

In a medium skillet over medium-high heat, heat the canola oil until almost smoking. Using tongs, dip a tortilla in the hot oil for a quick bath, about 4 seconds per side, then transfer to paper towels or a paper bag to drain while you repeat with the remaining tortillas.

Dip a tortilla into the bean mixture, coating it well on both sides. Place on an individual plate, sprinkle with a little cheese, and then fold in half. Sprinkle with a little more cheese and garnish with cilantro, if using, and a bit of the reserved onion. Repeat with the remaining tortillas, allowing 2 tortillas per serving. Top with a dollop of sour cream (if desired). Serve immediately.

MOLLETES
(MEXICAN BEANS ON TOAST)

Molletes are a traditional part of many Mexican breakfast tables. The rolls should be hearty or the bean spread can saturate them and make them unappealing. The fun is deciding the ratio of beans to bread—having a heavy hand isn't so bad. If you can't find Oaxaca cheese, any good melting cheese will be fine.

2 bolillo Mexican bread rolls (or French bread or ciabatta)

½ to 1 cup Glorious Refried Beans (page 61)

½ cup shredded queso Oaxaca (Oaxacan string cheese)

Salsa Fresca or Pantry Salsa (page 263) for serving

Cooked chorizo for serving (optional)

Fried eggs for serving (optional)

MAKES 2 TO 4 SERVINGS

Split the rolls in half lengthwise. Generously smear both halves of the rolls with refried beans. Sprinkle with cheese. Place each half on a baking pan with the bean-and-cheese side facing up.

Turn on your oven's broiler to its low setting. Place the baking pan on the middle rack and cook until the cheese starts to melt and brown on the edges, about 3 minutes.

Serve open-faced, topped with salsa and any other desired toppings.

BEANS ON TOAST

There is a very popular version of beans on toast in Britain. It's toasted bread with canned beans in a tomato sauce. It's a good way to get something on the table fast, but really, this dish can be more elevated. Those classic British beans, by the way, all come from North America.

Why not take a piece of fabulous rustic bread and make toast? It can even be past its prime since it will be toasted and adorned with good beans. Add some delicate white beans, a drizzle of olive oil, salt and pepper, maybe a dusting of Parmesan cheese, and you have a feast.

In Sorana, Italy, you'd use the local white bean, also called Sorana, and after spooning the beans over good toast, you'd gently drape a sheet of lardo over the top. Lardo is cured lard, and there is no substitute, but you might improvise with a very thinly sliced sheet of prosciutto crudo. Or maybe add a slice of ham to buttered bread, top with beans, and call that a meal.

One probably thinks mostly of white beans for this, but for molletes, a medium or dark bean is more common.

BEANS ON TOAST WITH POBLANOS AND QUESO FRESCO

This isn't a traditional dish, but roasted peppers, like Mexican poblanos or marinated red peppers, on good bread with beans and cheese is a good, quick dinner.

4 thick slices country-style bread

2 tablespoons (¼ stick) salted butter, at room temperature

2 poblano chiles, roasted, peeled, and seeded (see page 270), then cut into quarters

1 cup cooked, drained heirloom beans, such as Rancho Gordo Moro or Rebosero beans, warmed

½ cup crumbled queso fresco, mild feta, or farmer cheese

4 tablespoons extra-virgin olive oil

Salt

MAKES 4 SERVINGS

Toast the bread. Butter the toast and put a slice on each plate. Top each slice with 2 pieces of roasted chile, ¼ cup of beans, and 2 tablespoons of cheese. Drizzle each plate with 1 tablespoon of olive oil and finish with a sprinkle of salt.

Serve immediately.

ROASTED BROCCOLI RABE WITH WHITE BEANS AND PANCETTA

Broccoli rabe, or rapini, is a funny ingredient. It's somewhere between a vegetable and a green, like spinach or kale. It also is wildly bitter with touches of sweetness, especially when roasted. There are some who can't tolerate the bitterness, but most people will like its unusual flavor and how naturally it pairs with beans.

You can steam the broccoli rabe, but roasting really brings out the sweetness, and the texture is preferable with this method.

1 bunch broccoli rabe (about 1 pound), woody stems trimmed

3 tablespoons plus ¼ cup extra-virgin olive oil

Salt

4 ounces pancetta or bacon, cubed or chopped

2 garlic cloves, peeled and smashed

½ teaspoon red pepper flakes

2 cups cooked, drained white beans, such as Rancho Gordo Marcella, Royal Corona, or Cassoulet

Freshly ground pepper

Fresh lemon juice to taste

MAKES 2 TO 4 SERVINGS

Preheat the oven to 500°F.

Cut the broccoli rabe into thirds, then spread it out on a baking sheet and toss with 3 tablespoons of the olive oil. Season with salt. Roast the broccoli rabe for 5 minutes. Remove from the oven and carefully toss. Return to the oven and roast for another 5 minutes, until slightly charred and crisp-tender.

Meanwhile, in a large Dutch oven or other ovenproof skillet over medium-low heat, combine the remaining ¼ cup olive oil and the pancetta. Cook until the pancetta is browned and chewy, 10 to 15 minutes. Using a slotted spoon, remove the pancetta to paper towels and set aside. Decrease the heat, add the garlic and red pepper flakes, and sauté until the garlic is fragrant, 2 minutes. Add the beans and cook to heat through.

Add the broccoli rabe and reserved pancetta to the beans. Stir gently to combine. Season to taste with salt, pepper, and a squeeze of lemon.

VARIATION: VEGETARIAN ROASTED BROCCOLI RABE WITH WHITE BEANS

Omit the pancetta, and add a generous dusting of grated Parmesan cheese before serving.

CHIAPAS-STYLE GROUND BEEF, CABBAGE, AND WHITE BEANS

Food writer Diana Kennedy wrote about a delicious cabbage and ground beef dish she had in Chiapas, Mexico. It wasn't a typical regional dish, but it stayed with her enough to want to re-create it. We've simplified this quick, perfect weeknight dinner and added white beans to make it even richer. You could easily use darker beans or lighter ones. If you're concerned about aesthetics, black beans and green cabbage might look a little muddy and unappealing. You can easily use a purple cabbage and any bean you like, as long as it holds its shape after cooking.

3 garlic cloves, roughly chopped

6 whole peppercorns

Salt to taste

1 pound ground sirloin

3 tablespoons vegetable oil

¼ cup finely chopped white onion

1 jalapeño chile, seeded and finely chopped

1 medium tomato (about 6 ounces), finely chopped, or ½ cup canned diced tomatoes

4 cups finely shredded cabbage

1½ cups cooked, drained white beans, such as Rancho Gordo Ayocote Blanco beans

⅔ cup water

½ cup roughly chopped fresh cilantro, firmly packed

Tostadas or cooked rice for serving

MAKES 4 SERVINGS

Using a mortar and pestle, crush the garlic, peppercorns, and salt together. In a bowl, combine the sirloin and garlic mixture and mix well. Set aside for a few minutes to season.

Heat the oil in a large, heavy skillet over medium heat. Add the onion, jalapeño, and a sprinkle of salt and cook until the onion is translucent, about 1 minute. Add the tomato and cook until most of the juice has been absorbed, about 3 minutes.

Add the beef to the pan and cook, stirring from time to time, until the meat is browned, about 7 minutes. Add the cabbage, beans, water, and cilantro and cook, stirring from time to time, until the mixture is well seasoned and moist but not juicy, about 15 minutes.

Serve on tostadas or with rice. It also makes a delicious stuffing for chiles.

ROASTED CHICKEN THIGHS OVER POBLANO AND WHITE BEAN SAUCE

Poblano chiles are large, mostly mild green chiles that are very common in Mexican cooking. They are thick and meaty and have an oddly appealing earthy flavor. The standard preparation, called Rajas con Crema, is to roast them, let them rest and steam, skin them, and then deseed before using. After cutting up the strips, you fry them with onion and garlic and then toss them in heavy cream—and, yes, it's just about as delicious as it sounds. Poblanos are also prepared stuffed (chiles rellenos) or, as in this recipe, pureed into a sauce. The versatile sauce also pairs well with shrimp or fish, roasted vegetables, or even pasta with Parmesan, cracked pepper, and a drizzle of olive oil.

FOR THE CHICKEN
4 to 6 bone-in, skin-on chicken thighs

¼ cup extra-virgin olive oil, plus more for the roasting pan

Salt and freshly ground pepper

FOR THE SAUCE
3 tablespoons extra-virgin olive oil

½ white onion, chopped

2 garlic cloves, minced

4 poblano chiles, roasted, peeled, and seeded (see page 270)

1 cup cooked, drained white beans, such as Rancho Gordo Alubia Blanca or Marcella beans

¼ cup beer or half-and-half, or as needed

Small bunch fresh epazote leaves, chopped (optional)

Corn kernels from 1 ear of corn

MAKES 4 SERVINGS

Preheat the oven to 400°F.

To make the chicken: In a bowl, combine the chicken, olive oil, and salt and pepper to taste. Toss well and arrange, skin-side up, in an oiled roasting pan. Roast for 30 to 40 minutes, until the skin is browned and an instant-read thermometer inserted into the thickest part of the thighs reaches 165°F.

To make the sauce: Meanwhile, in a medium skillet over medium-low heat, warm the olive oil. Add the onion and garlic and cook until softened, about 10 minutes.

In a blender, combine the chiles and beans and just enough beer to make the blades move and blend well. Puree until smooth.

Add the blended sauce to the onion mixture. Add more beer if needed to reach the desired consistency. Increase the heat to medium and cook, stirring, for 10 minutes. Add the epazote (if using), corn, and salt to taste, and continue to cook until the corn is tender, another 5 or so minutes.

Spoon some of the sauce on a serving platter or individual plates, then top with the chicken. Serve additional sauce on the side.

MILD BEANS WITH OUR FAVORITE TOPPINGS

Here's the basic recipe: Cook a simple pot of beans, and for each bowl, add a healthy dollop of one of the following toppings. There's a good chance you'll have made some of them already, but all of them work with a bowl of beans, and maybe later as a pasta sauce or even a part of a mixed salad.

FRIED RICOTTA

1 tablespoon extra-virgin olive oil

½ cup minced onion

2 cups ricotta, drained

1 teaspoon salt

¼ cup chopped fresh epazote (optional)

1 tablespoon finely chopped serrano or jalapeño chile

MAKES ABOUT 2 CUPS

In a large skillet over medium-high heat, warm the olive oil. Add the onion and cook until translucent, about 3 minutes.

Add the ricotta and cook, breaking up clumps with a wooden spoon, until most of the moisture is gone, 8 to 10 minutes. Stir in the salt. Remove from the heat. Stir in the epazote (if using) and chopped chile.

RAJAS (POBLANO STRIPS)

2 tablespoons olive oil

½ white onion, thinly sliced

1 garlic clove, minced

1 teaspoon dried Mexican oregano, preferably Rancho Gordo Oregano Indio

2 poblano chiles, roasted (see page 270) and sliced into strips

Salt to taste

MAKES ABOUT 1 CUP

In a large skillet over medium-low heat, warm the olive oil. Add the onion, garlic, and oregano and cook until the onion is soft, about 10 minutes. Add the chiles and stir to combine. Cook until heated through, about 5 minutes. Season with salt.

CARAMELIZED ONIONS OR LEEKS

2 tablespoons (¼ stick) butter

2 tablespoons olive oil

2 yellow onions or sweet onions, halved, then thinly sliced, or 4 leeks, white and light green parts only, sliced and rinsed thoroughly

½ teaspoon salt, or to taste

MAKES ABOUT ½ CUP

In a large, heavy skillet over medium heat, warm the butter with the olive oil. Add the onions and cook, stirring often, until golden and soft, about 30 minutes. Decrease the heat if needed to avoid burning. Add about 1 tablespoon of water and stir, scraping up the bits on the bottom and sides of the pan. Use additional water if needed. Stir in salt. Continue to cook until the onions are brown and jammy, another 15 to 20 minutes.

ITALIAN SALSA VERDE

1½ cups mixed fresh herbs, such as flat-leaf parsley, oregano, rosemary, thyme, and sage

¼ cup capers, drained

½ cup extra-virgin olive oil

Zest and juice of 1 lemon

Sea salt and freshly ground pepper

MAKES ABOUT ½ CUP

On a cutting board, mince all of the herbs together. Add the capers and mince again. Transfer to a bowl and whisk in the olive oil, lemon zest, and lemon juice. Season with salt and pepper. (You can also prepare in a food processor.)

PICKLED SHALLOTS

3 shallots, thinly sliced

½ jalapeño, seeded and thinly sliced (optional)

Banana vinegar, pineapple vinegar, or unseasoned rice vinegar

Pinch of sea salt

½ teaspoon dried Mexican oregano, preferably Rancho Gordo Oregano Indio, plus more for garnish

MAKES ABOUT ¼ CUP

In a glass or ceramic bowl, combine the shallots and jalapeño (if using). Add enough banana vinegar to cover completely. Season with a pinch of salt. Crush the oregano with your hands, and add it as well. Let marinate for about 15 minutes, stirring occasionally. Garnish with additional oregano.

PICKLED CHILES

1 cup distilled white vinegar, rice vinegar, or pineapple vinegar, plus more as needed

½ cup water, plus more as needed

1 bay leaf

½ teaspoon dried Mexican oregano, preferably Rancho Gordo Oregano Indio

1 garlic clove, smashed

1 sprig thyme or marjoram

2 teaspoons sea salt

10 jalapeño chiles, stems removed, sliced

MAKES ABOUT 1 CUP WITH LIQUID

In a medium saucepan over high heat, combine the white vinegar, water, bay leaf, oregano, garlic, thyme, and salt. Bring to a boil. Decrease the heat to a gentle simmer and cook for 5 minutes. Turn off the heat.

In a medium glass or ceramic bowl, combine the chile slices with the vinegar mixture. Add more vinegar and water in equal parts, as needed, to cover the chiles. Allow to cool, then cover and refrigerate for at least 4 hours. Remove the bay leaf before serving.

LEMON-CAPER SAUCE

2 anchovy fillets, chopped (optional)

¾ cup chopped fresh flat-leaf parsley

1 garlic clove, minced

1 tablespoon capers, chopped

Zest and juice from 1 lemon, plus more as needed

½ cup extra-virgin olive oil

Freshly ground pepper

Salt to taste (optional)

MAKES ABOUT ½ CUP

Place the chopped anchovies (if using) on a cutting board and, using the blade of a large chef's knife, mash them against the board until you have a rough paste, or use a mortar and pestle. In a mixing bowl, combine the anchovy paste, parsley, garlic, capers, lemon zest, lemon juice, olive oil, and pepper. Gently mix and taste for seasoning. Add salt if necessary. The sauce should be strong and aggressive as it will be tossed with mild beans. Depending on your taste, you may want to add more lemon juice.

ANCHO CHILES RELLENOS SMOTHERED IN TOMATO SAUCE

Ancho chiles are dried poblano chiles. The rich, juicy chile becomes dense and raisiny when dried, and it's very versatile. Mostly they're used in classic sauces. Mexicans lightly toast, hydrate in warm water, seed, puree, "fry," and then thin out with stock or water for a classic sauce, often with other chiles, like guajillos, thrown in to brighten things up. This recipe simplifies things in that you'll just be hydrating and seeding and then stuffing with refried beans and cheese. This is based on a recipe from Guadalupe Romero Vidal, and the result is out of this world!

FOR THE TOMATO SAUCE

3 white or yellow onion slices with the skins on

2 garlic cloves, unpeeled

1 canela stick (true cinnamon)

3 or 4 canned whole peeled tomatoes, plus about ¼ cup juice reserved

1 teaspoon Mexican oregano, preferably Rancho Gordo Oregano Indio

Chicken or vegetable stock, if needed

2 tablespoons olive oil or lard (manteca)

Salt to taste

4 large, pliable ancho chiles, wiped clean (avoid hard/brittle chiles)

4 cups hot (not boiling) water

1 tablespoon pineapple vinegar or apple cider vinegar

To make the tomato sauce: In a comal or cast-iron skillet over medium heat, char the onion slices and garlic until soft, about 10 minutes. Remove from the heat and allow to cool to the touch. Char the canela stick over an open flame, turning often, for about 2 minutes. The stick should give off its aroma. Set aside. Peel off the onion and garlic skins and discard.

In a blender, combine the tomatoes, reserved tomato juice, oregano, onion, and garlic. Blend until smooth, adding a little stock if the blades get stuck.

In a large pan, heat the olive oil over medium heat. Add the tomato mixture and the canela and "fry," stirring constantly. Simmer gently, stirring constantly, until the sauce has thickened, about 15 minutes. Season with salt. Remove and discard the canela stick. Use the sauce as is or thin with more stock.

To make the chiles rellenos: Place the chiles in a large, wide bowl. Add hot water to cover and then add the vinegar. Use a plate or tongs to keep the chiles submerged as they rehydrate, 5 to 10 minutes (depending on how dry they are). They should be soft and pliable.

1 cup cooked, drained medium-bodied beans, such as Rancho Gordo Rebosero, Pinto, or Mayocoba (preferably refried, see page 61)

1 cup shredded Chihuahua melting cheese, Oaxaca melting cheese, or mozzarella cheese

1 tablespoon olive oil or lard (manteca)

4 tablespoons Mexican crema or sour cream thinned with water or lime juice, for serving

MAKES 4 STUFFED CHILES

Remove the chiles from the water and place on a cutting board. Using a sharp knife, make a small horizontal slit across the top of a chile just below the stem, leaving the stem intact. Starting from the middle of the slit, slice lengthwise down to the tip of the chile (make sure you cut through only one layer). Open the chile and pull out the seeds and inner membranes. Repeat with the remaining chiles. Once cleaned, pat the chiles dry with paper towels.

Carefully stuff each chile with ¼ cup of the beans and then ¼ cup of the cheese. Close up the slits as best you can. The melted cheese will act as a glue to keep the slits closed.

In a medium skillet or comal over medium heat, warm the oil. Add the chiles and cook, carefully flipping them once, until the cheese is melted and the chiles are slightly seared, 2 to 3 minutes per side.

Place warm tomato sauce on each plate and top with the chiles rellenos. Drizzle about 1 tablespoon of crema over the top of each chile.

ROASTED CABBAGE WEDGES WITH WILD MUSHROOMS AND HEIRLOOM BEANS

Roasting cabbage wedges at high heat completely transforms them from a utilitarian vegetable to something sublime. Serving cabbage with brothy heirloom beans makes for a complete, delicious, simple meal.

There are several ways of roasting cabbage. Some people prefer slices, like steaks, and others cook the cabbage whole. Our wedges are inspired by writer Allison Robicelli.

8 ounces fresh mushrooms, preferably wild

½ cup olive oil

2 garlic cloves, sliced

Salt

1 whole cabbage, sliced into thick wedges

Freshly ground pepper

½ lemon

2 cups cooked, drained medium-bodied heirloom beans, such as Rancho Gordo Buckeye, King City Pink, or Santa Maria Pinquito, plus 1½ to 2 cups bean broth reserved

Italian Salsa Verde (page 246) for serving (optional)

MAKES 2 TO 4 SERVINGS

Wipe the mushrooms clean with a cloth or brush. Cut off and discard the end of the stems, then roughly chop. In a medium skillet over medium-high heat, warm ¼ cup of the olive oil. Add the mushrooms and garlic and cook, stirring, until the mushrooms are soft and fragrant, 10 to 12 minutes. Turn off the heat and season with salt.

Preheat the oven to 500°F.

In a large bowl, gently toss the cabbage wedges with the remaining ¼ cup olive oil and salt to taste. Place on a parchment-lined baking sheet. Roast the cabbage for 10 minutes; remove the baking sheet from the oven, flip the wedges, and return to roast for another 10 minutes. The edges of the cabbage should be a little crisp and caramelized. Remove from the oven, sprinkle with pepper, and add a squeeze of lemon.

Gently stir the beans and broth into the cooked mushrooms and cook over medium-low heat until heated through.

Serve the cabbage wedges alongside the warm beans and mushrooms. Top with salsa verde (if desired).

SWEETS, STOCKS, SALSAS & MORE

As a child in the San Francisco Bay Area, I remember craving bean pie from Your Black Muslim Bakery even more than It's-It ice cream sandwiches. I would never say no to an It's-It, but my heart belonged to the super-smooth bean filling used in those pies. If you're a Bean Person, you're probably curious—and I promise they won't disappoint!

Beyond the sweets in this chapter, there are several delicious salsas, two kinds of cornbread, some foundational stocks, and methods for roasting peppers and making croutons. I make chicken stock nearly every weekend. With minimal fuss, I get enough cooked chicken for several meals and nearly a gallon of delicious chicken broth. The same idea goes for vegetable stock. Save up the vegetable odds and ends in your crisper—leek tops, wilted herbs, onion parts, celery tops—and simmer them in water for a rich, flavorful liquid you can use throughout the week. Nothing goes to waste, and you benefit from it with little hands-on work. My recipe for Pantry Salsa follows a similar strategy: combine a few ingredients you probably already have in your pantry and refrigerator for a homemade, fresh salsa that rivals any you'd purchase from the store in a plastic container. Once you get the hang of it, you'll wonder why you ever bought premade salsa.

YOUR BLACK MUSLIM BAKERY
NAVY BEAN PIE

Residents of the San Francisco Bay Area will remember these pies from Your Black Muslim Bakery. Weird, wonderful, and reminiscent of sweet potato pie, the classic recipe uses white beans, but there are variations with pinto or black beans.

Make sure you blend well for a silky texture.

2 cups cooked, drained, and mashed Rancho Gordo Alubia Blanca beans, navy beans, or other white beans, prepared without salt

2 eggs, lightly beaten

¾ cup evaporated milk

¾ cup sugar

1 teaspoon ground cinnamon

1 teaspoon ground nutmeg

½ teaspoon ground ginger

¼ teaspoon ground clove

½ teaspoon salt

1 teaspoon vanilla extract

1 unbaked 9-inch pie shell

Whipped cream (optional)

MAKES ONE 9-INCH PIE

Preheat the oven to 400°F.

In the bowl of a stand mixer, or in a bowl with an electric hand mixer, beat the beans well. Add the eggs and evaporated milk and beat until smooth. Add the sugar, cinnamon, nutmeg, ginger, clove, salt, and vanilla. Beat at medium speed until well blended and smooth.

Carefully pour the mixture into the unbaked pie shell. Bake for 10 minutes. Decrease the heat to 350°F and bake for another 35 minutes, or until a knife inserted in the center comes out clean.

Serve warm or at room temperature, with whipped cream if you'd like.

TEXAS PINTOS AND HONEY

Texans laugh at us and say this dish doesn't exist in their state, but chili con carne expert Frank X. Tolbert describes a nice bowl of pinto beans with honey. It's really tasty and would be something fun to try when you're camping.

3 cups cooked pinto beans, bean broth reserved, prepared with a minimal amount of salt

1 to 2 tablespoons good-quality honey, plus more for serving

Cornbread for serving
(see page 264 or 265)

MAKES 4 TO 6 SERVINGS

In a medium pot over medium heat, warm the pintos in their broth. When the beans are warm, divide them among bowls and drizzle each bowl with about 1 teaspoon of honey. Serve with hot cornbread. Pass additional honey at the table.

DULCE DE FRIJOL NORTEÑO

Bean pudding might sound a little odd, but like the navy bean pie on page 257, you've got to try beans in a sweet dish. Dulce de Frijol is a regional dish in Mexico. In some areas, the beans are cooked with canela, orange juice, and sugar to a paste-like consistency, and then formed into balls. This version, which originated in northern Mexico, is more like a pudding. It takes a good while for the mixture to thicken—possibly longer than it takes to cook a pot of beans!

½ gallon whole milk

2 cups cooked, drained medium-bodied beans, such as bayo beans or Rancho Gordo Pinto beans, prepared without salt

1½ cups sugar

2 canela sticks (true cinnamon)

3 egg yolks

¼ cup cornstarch, mixed with a splash of milk or water to remove lumps

½ cup chopped toasted almonds

½ cup chopped toasted walnuts (optional)

MAKES 4 TO 6 SERVINGS

Using a blender or immersion blender, blend the milk with the beans. Strain the mixture into a saucepan and add the sugar and canela. Cook over medium heat, stirring frequently to avoid scorching, until the mixture starts to thicken, about 1 to 1½ hours.

Remove from the heat. Add a small amount of the warm milk mixture to the egg yolks and mix well to temper them, then slowly whisk the eggs into the pot, followed by the cornstarch and almonds. Over medium-low heat, cook stirring frequently, until the mixture is thick enough that you can drag a wooden spoon across the bottom of the pan and it leaves a clear trail, another hour or so.

Remove from the heat and discard the canela sticks. Spoon into small bowls and garnish with walnuts, if desired. You can also enjoy it chilled: let the pudding cool, then transfer to a bowl and refrigerate for at least 1 hour.

DE ÁRBOL CHILE SALSA

De árbol chiles are small, fiery chiles used often in Mexican cooking. A good de árbol will be very spicy, but they also have a nice nutty flavor. You might want to warn your guests before serving this salsa: it's seriously spicy! Feel free to decrease the amount of chiles to suit your taste.

¼ to ½ cup dried chiles de árbol, wiped clean with a moist towel, stems removed

1 Roma tomato

2 tablespoons pineapple vinegar or apple cider vinegar

Juice of 2 Mexican limes or key limes (about 1 tablespoon)

¼ teaspoon ground cumin

1 garlic clove, peeled

Salt to taste

MAKES ABOUT ½ CUP

Warm a dry comal or small skillet over medium heat. Add the chiles and toast them quickly, taking care not to let them burn. Remove the chiles and set them aside. Add the tomatoes to the comal and char until the skin is blackened and the inside is soft, 15 to 20 minutes.

In a bowl, combine the chiles, pineapple vinegar, and lime juice. Let the chiles hydrate for 15 minutes. In a blender, process the chiles and their soaking liquid, tomato, cumin, and garlic until smooth. Add a little water if needed to keep the blades moving. Push the mixture through a fine-mesh sieve into a small bowl, discarding the skins and seeds. Taste and add salt, as desired.

SALSA VERDE IN A MOLCAJETE

If you have a molcajete (the traditional Mexican version of a mortar and pestle, made from volcanic rock), chances are it too often sits idle. What a shame! Making a simple green salsa in a molcajete is easy, and your salsa will have a wonderful, authentic texture that you can't get from any other method. If you don't have a molcajete, you can make use of a food processor.

5 or 6 medium tomatillos

1 large slice white onion, finely chopped

4 serrano chiles, finely minced

3 garlic cloves, finely minced

Salt

1 teaspoon dried Mexican oregano, preferably Rancho Gordo Oregano Indio

Juice of ½ lime

Small handful of fresh cilantro, finely chopped

MAKES ABOUT ¾ CUP

Rinse and dry the tomatillos and then roast them on a hot, dry skillet or comal, rotating them often so they have nice charred spots but don't burn. They should be soft in about 5 to 8 minutes.

Meanwhile, in a molcajete, combine the onion, chiles, garlic, and salt to taste. Mash until they are broken down and blended. The finer your initial chop, the less work this will be.

When the tomatillos are soft and hissing, remove them from the heat and allow to cool. Finely chop them and add to the molcajete. Start grinding again. Add the oregano, lime juice, and cilantro and combine.

PANTRY SALSA

When in-season tomatoes and tomatillos are not handy, my standby is this salsa that uses ingredients that can be found in your pantry, giving you no excuse to buy commercial salsa!

½ red onion, roughly chopped

3 garlic cloves, roughly chopped

1 cup canned tomatoes

¼ cup chopped chiles, such as jalapeño or serrano, canned or fresh, or to taste

Salt to taste

3 tablespoons pineapple vinegar or lime juice, or to taste

¼ cup chopped fresh cilantro or flat-leaf parsley (optional)

MAKES ABOUT 1 CUP

Place all the ingredients in the bowl of a food processor and pulse until just chopped.

BOETTICHER FAMILY CORNBREAD

My pal Taylor Boetticher of the Fatted Calf loves chili con carne. If you think Texans are passionate about their chili, you should hear them rant about cornbread. From Taylor, via his mother (thank you, Ma'am!), here is the Boetticher family cornbread recipe.

2 tablespoons (¼ stick) unsalted butter

1⅓ cups yellow cornmeal

⅓ cup flour

3 tablespoons sugar

1 teaspoon salt

1 teaspoon baking soda

2 cups milk

1 cup buttermilk

2 large eggs

MAKES 4 TO 6 SERVINGS

Preheat the oven to 400°F.

Place the butter in a 9- or 10-inch cast-iron skillet and place in the oven for 5 minutes.

Meanwhile, in a large bowl, mix the cornmeal, flour, sugar, salt, and baking soda. Stir in 1 cup of the milk and the buttermilk. Add the eggs and blend thoroughly. Pour the batter into the hot skillet and carefully pour the remaining 1 cup milk into the batter. Don't worry that it looks too runny. DO NOT STIR. The milk will sink and form a custard-like layer. Bake until golden, 30 to 35 minutes. Serve while hot.

STEVE'S SKILLET CORNBREAD

I am a fan of corn in all of its forms, and recently I got obsessed with making cornbread. Aside from corn tortillas, cornbread may be the best friend a bowl of beans ever had. My favorite version doesn't call for flour. I prefer the rustic texture of the cornmeal and the slight tang from the yogurt. I am not shy when slathering soft butter on warm cornbread, and you shouldn't be, either.

4 tablespoons (½ stick) butter

1½ cups cornmeal

½ teaspoon baking soda

½ teaspoon salt

1 cup milk

1 tablespoon yogurt or sour cream

1 large egg

MAKES 4 TO 6 SERVINGS

Preheat the oven to 400°F.

In a 9- or 10-inch cast-iron skillet over low heat, melt the butter.

In a mixing bowl, mix together the cornmeal, baking soda, and salt. Add the milk, yogurt, and egg, and stir until all the ingredients are incorporated.

Add the batter to the skillet, transfer to the oven, and bake until golden, about 20 minutes.

CREAMY POLENTA

A bowl of hot, creamy polenta is magical, and it makes the perfect bed for beans. This recipe is adapted from Anson Mills, a North Carolina–based company that produces heirloom grains. They mill and ship their ground new-crop corn once a week.

1 cup uncooked fine yellow polenta, preferably Anson Mills

3½ cups water

3 tablespoons grated Parmesan cheese

2 tablespoons (¼ stick) unsalted butter

1 teaspoon salt

Freshly ground pepper

MAKES 2 TO 4 SERVINGS

In a heavy-bottomed pot, combine the polenta with the water. Bring to a simmer over medium-high heat, stirring constantly with a wooden spoon, until the mixture begins to thicken, 5 to 8 minutes. Decrease the heat to the lowest setting and cook with the pot lid slightly ajar, stirring frequently, until the grains are soft and hold their shape on a spoon, 35 to 40 minutes. Whisk in the cheese, butter, salt, and a few grinds of pepper.

POACHED EGGS

There are very few bean dishes that don't benefit from a poached egg.

1 tablespoon white vinegar

2 to 4 eggs

Fill a medium saucepan with water and add the white vinegar. Heat the water over medium heat. When the water is barely simmering, carefully crack the eggs and slide them one at a time into the water (or you can crack them into a bowl first and then gently tip the bowl over the hot water). Cook until the whites are just set and the yolks are still soft, 2 to 3 minutes.

HOMEMADE CROUTONS

Start making homemade croutons and your bread never goes to waste. Pack them in an airtight container, and you'll be happy to have them on hand for bean salads, soups, and casseroles.

4 slices crusty or stale bread

2 tablespoons olive oil

1 teaspoon salt

MAKES ABOUT 4 CUPS (DEPENDING ON THE SIZE OF YOUR BREAD)

Preheat the oven to 400°F.

Remove the crust from the bread if you like, then tear or cut it into 1-inch pieces. On a baking sheet, toss the bread with the olive oil and salt. Bake the bread until it's golden and toasted, 10 to 15 minutes, checking and shaking the pan every 5 minutes or so.

CHICKEN STOCK

1 whole bone-in chicken breast with skin on

2 chicken feet

Vegetable scraps, such as onion tops, little garlic cloves, corn silk, or celery

¼ yellow or white onion, sliced

4 to 6 garlic cloves, cut in half

3 bay leaves

3 whole peppercorns

Salt to taste

MAKES 6 TO 8 CUPS STOCK, PLUS ABOUT 2 CUPS SHREDDED CHICKEN

Place the chicken breast and feet in a large stockpot and add water to cover by ½ inch. Turn the heat to high. Once the water starts to boil, decrease the heat to medium-low to maintain a gentle simmer. After about 5 minutes, check for scum on top of the water and remove with a small sieve or slotted spoon. Add the rest of the broth ingredients and continue simmering, partially covered, until the chicken pieces are cooked through, about 20 minutes.

Allow the chicken pieces to cool. Remove any remaining skin and shred the meat with your hands. Strain the broth using cheesecloth placed over a fine-mesh sieve and discard the solids.

SEAFOOD STOCK

2 to 3 cups shrimp shells, fish bones, and/or fish heads

1 small white onion, quartered

2 celery stalks, roughly chopped

4 garlic cloves

1 teaspoon dried Mexican oregano, preferably Rancho Gordo Oregano Indio (optional)

1 tablespoon fish sauce (optional)

8 cups water

MAKES ABOUT 6 CUPS

In a pot, combine the seafood pieces with the onion, celery, garlic, oregano (if using), and fish sauce (if using). Add the water and bring to a boil. Decrease the heat and simmer for about 30 minutes.

Strain the broth using cheesecloth placed over a fine-mesh sieve and discard the solids.

VEGETABLE STOCK

About 2 cups vegetable scraps, such as carrots, celery, fennel, onion, or leek

4 to 6 garlic cloves

1 bay leaf

A handful of peppercorns

8 cups water

MAKES 4 TO 6 CUPS

In a pot, combine the vegetables, garlic, bay leaf, and peppercorns with the water. Bring to a boil, then decrease the heat and simmer, partially covered, for 45 minutes to 1 hour. Let the broth cool a bit in the pot, then strain the broth using cheesecloth placed over a fine-mesh sieve and discard the solids.

CORN STOCK

8 to 10 corncobs, kernels removed and reserved for another use

Silk from 2 corncobs (optional)

5 peppercorns

½ white onion

Handful of fresh parsley

2 sprigs thyme

1 bay leaf

10 cups cold water

MAKES 6 TO 8 CUPS

In a large pot, combine the corncobs, silk (if using), peppercorns, onion, parsley, thyme, bay leaf, and cold water and bring to a boil over high heat. Decrease the heat to low, partially cover, and simmer for about 40 minutes, or until the desired flavor is reached. Strain the broth using cheesecloth placed over a fine-mesh sieve and discard the solids.

ROASTED PEPPERS

The technique for roasting peppers in Italy and Mexico is almost the same. In Mexico, you'd roast mostly poblano peppers, and in Italy, it seems red peppers are the most common.

Roasted peppers add color and flavor to bean salads, such as Big White Beans with Roasted Peppers and Pepitas (page 88) or Garbanzo Salad with Spanish Chorizo and Red Peppers (page 102). You can also puree them in sauces (see page 242) or drape them over beans on toast (see page 238).

Roasting on a gas range: Roast the peppers directly on the grate over medium-high heat, using flameproof tongs to turn the peppers as they char. It's best to keep them moving. The goal is to char the skins, which will cook the pepper perfectly. You can also roast the peppers on a hot cast-iron skillet or steel comal, turning the peppers as the skins char.

Roasting in the oven: Preheat the oven to 400°F. Line a baking sheet with a Silpat mat, parchment paper, or aluminum foil, then add whole peppers and roast them for 20 to 30 minutes, turning occasionally, until the skins are charred all over.

Roasting with a handheld burner: If you are obsessive (and what's wrong with that?), consider a handheld butane torch, like the Bernzomatic model. The Bernzomatic is also great for crème brûlée. You can roast using your preferred method and then use the handheld torch to go into the crevices that you may have missed, especially if you're roasting on a pan or in the oven.

Once your peppers or chiles are roasted, steam them to help release the skins. A lot of recipes will suggest a plastic bag, but the idea of hot peppers in plastic is unappealing. Hot plastic is always off-putting. You can let the peppers rest for about 20 minutes in a paper bag, rolled at the top to keep the steam in, or simply place the peppers in a mixing bowl and cover them with a large dinner plate.

After 20 minutes, scrape off the skins, pull open the peppers, and remove the seeds and stems. Chop and use as desired. Our favorite is to let them luxuriate in good olive oil.

ACKNOWLEDGMENTS

This book is dedicated to home cooks everywhere.

No one does this alone. We'd like to thank those who agreed to contribute a recipe and also those who inspired us with an idea or technique: Emma Lipp, Pamela Sheldon Johns, Jeremy Fox, José Rivelino D. Santos Silva, Staffan Terje, Heidi Swanson, Najmieh Batmanglij, Julia Heffelfinger, Faith Kramer, Alexis Handelman, Celene Cisneros, Arnab Chakladar, Deb Perelman, Sarah Scott, Margaret Roach, Michael Gyetvan, Guadalupe Romero Vidal, Laura Wright, Joshua McFadden, Marcella Hazan, Judith Barrett, José Pizarro, Michelle McDonnell, Diane Kochilas, Paula Wolfert, Diana Kennedy, Allison Robicelli, Frank X. Tolbert, Judy Witts Francini, Thomas Keller, Sam and Sam Clark, Joan Smith, Kate Hill, Georgeanne Brennan, Ken Albala, and Dan Buettner.

We'd also like to thank: Yunuen Carrillo, Gabriel Cortes, Lukas Volger, Ethan Frisch, Ori Zohar, Peter Miller, Scott Peacock, Tracy Ryder, Delilah Snell, Gustavo Arellano, Carolyn Tillie, Carrie Brown, Constance Green, Emily Nunn, Joan Crowley, Joe McConnell, John Monks, Kathy Stevenson, Maureen and Mike Crumly, Glen Fishman, Nico Sando, Bobbi Sando, Toponia Miller, Taylor Boetticher, Efren and Debora Pelayo, Eileen and Rich Pharo, Marge Caldwell, Michael Mascioli, Mike Greensill, Sarah Lonsdale, Gina Yoshida, Kyle Corsiglia, Dana and Jackson Ratcliffe, Robert Stephens, Gail Wadsworth, Moises Plascencia, and the Rancho Gordo staff, one and all, but special thanks to the test kitchen crew who made this book possible: Nancy Aguilar, Diana Arriaga, Celene Cisneros, Monica Casillas Gutierrez, and Lisa Nunez-Hancock.

Thank you to José Andrés, Ted Allen, Tanya Holland, and Evan Kleiman for your support.

And of course, the creative crew at Ten Speed Press who made this book a reality: Lorena Jones, Kim Keller, Emma Campion, Ed Anderson, Lillian Kang, Paige Arnett, Abby Oladipo, Mari Gill, Kim Tyner, David Hawk, Monica Stanton, and Allison Renzulli.

INDEX

Typefaces: URW Type Foundry's Berling and Latinotype's Texta.

Library of Congress Cataloging-in-Publication Data
Names: Sando, Steve, author.
Title: The bean book : 100 recipes for cooking with all kinds of beans,
    from the rancho gordo kitchen / by Steve Sando.
Identifiers: LCCN 2023048225 (print) | LCCN 2023048226 (ebook) | ISBN
9781984860002 (hardcover) | ISBN 9781984860019 (ebook)
Subjects: LCSH: Cooking (Beans) | LCGFT: Cookbooks.
Classification: LCC TX803.B4 S259 2024 (print) | LCC TX803.B4 (ebook) |
    DDC 641.6/565—dc23/eng/20240126
LC record available at https://lccn.loc.gov/2023048225
LC ebook record available at https://lccn.loc.gov/2023048226

ISBN: 978-1-9848-6000-2
Ebook ISBN: 978-1-9848-6001-9

Printed in China

Acquiring editor: Lorena Jones | Project editor: Kim Keller | Production editor: Abby Oladipo
Designer: Ashley Lima | Art director: Emma Campion | Production designers: Mari Gill and Faith Hague
Cover design: Emma Campion
Production manager: Kim Tyner
Food & prop stylist: Lillian Kang | Food stylist assistant: Paige Arnett
Copyeditor: Amy Kovalski | Proofreader: Michelle Hubner | Indexer: Thérèse Shere
Publicist: David Hawk | Marketers: Monica Stanton and Allison Renzulli

10 9 8 7 6 5 4 3 2 1

First Edition

BEAN CONVERSIONS

 =  =

1 pound
dried beans

2 cups dried
beans

about 6 cups
cooked beans

 =

1 cup dried
beans

about 3 cups
cooked beans

 =

1 (15-ounce) can
of beans

about 1 ½ cups
cooked beans

 =

1 pound
dried beans

4 (15-ounce)
cans of beans